Judgement Day

JUDGEMENT DAY

haiku, senryu,
& other aimless utterances by

Gabriel Rosenstock

collages by

Karl Waldmann

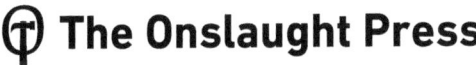 **The Onslaught Press**

Published in Oxford by The Onslaught Press
11 Ridley Road, OX4 2QJ
August 2016

Unless otherwise stated, all texts © 2016 **Gabriel Rosenstock**
Gabriel Rosenstock asserts his moral right to be identified as the author of this book

Cover © 2016 **Mathew Staunton**

All images in this book belong to the **Karl Waldmann Museum**,
108 ch. de Charleroi, 1060 Brussels, Belgium,
0032 (0) 2 5378136
www.karlwaldmannmuseum.com
and are published here with their generous authorization

ISBN: **978-0-9934217-8-5**

Typeset by Mathew Staunton in **DIN Next** (interior) and **MICROBREW** (cover)
Printed and bound by Lightning Source

lá bhreithe dé
séid an troimpéad sin—
séid glé os ard

judgement day
blow that horn—
blow loud and clear

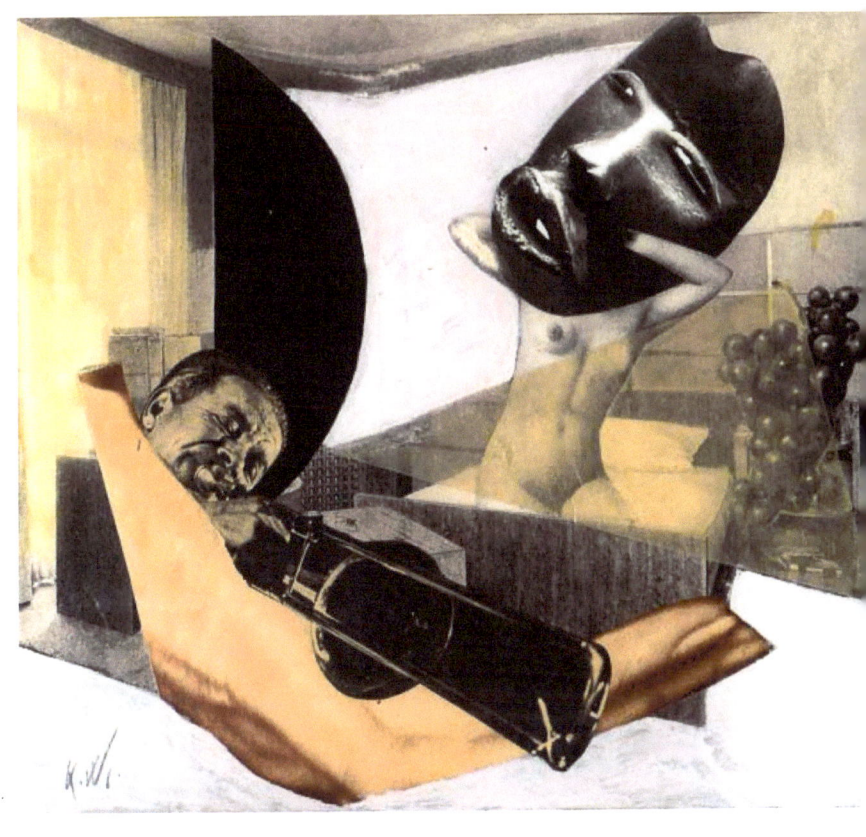

croch bun os cionn—
d'fhonn radharc níos fearr
a fháil ar an domhan

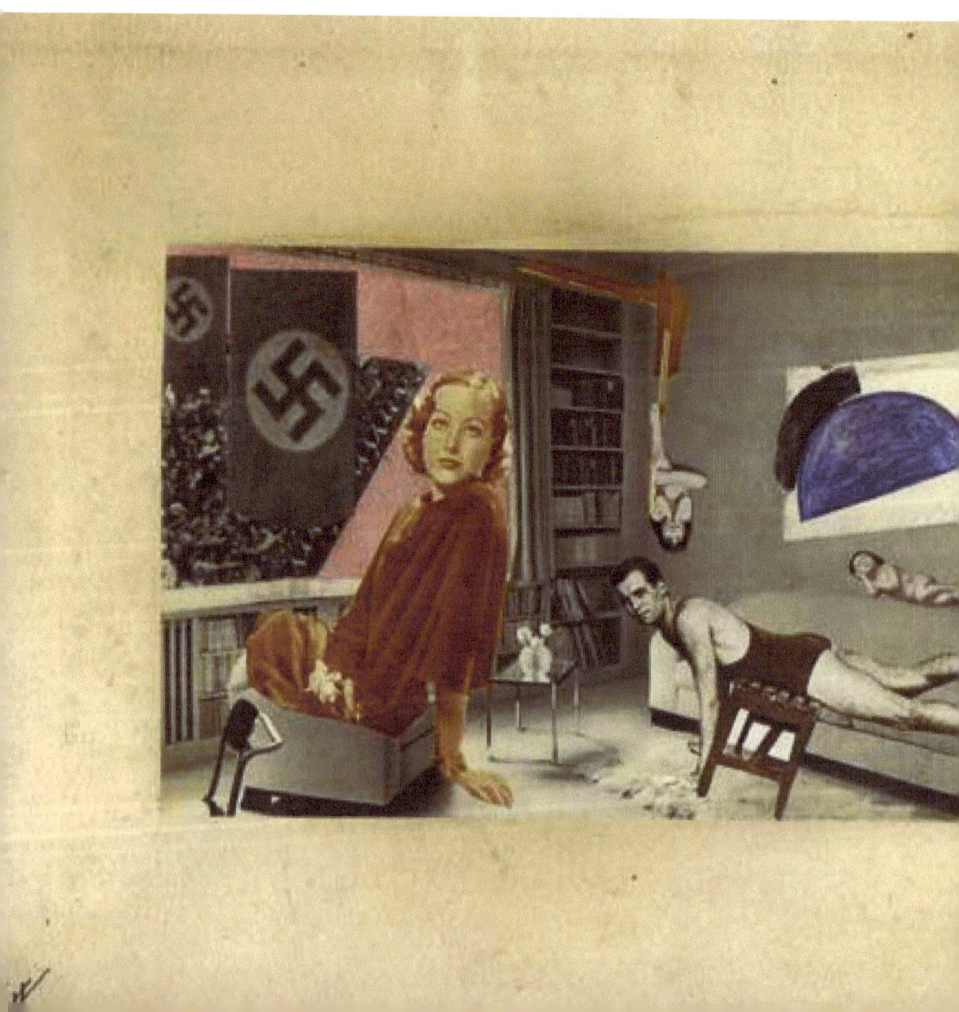

hang upside down—
for a much better view of
the world

os cionn na ngort cruithneachta
san úcráin—
fuiseog ag canadh di féin

over the wheat fields
of ukraine—
a lark singing to itself

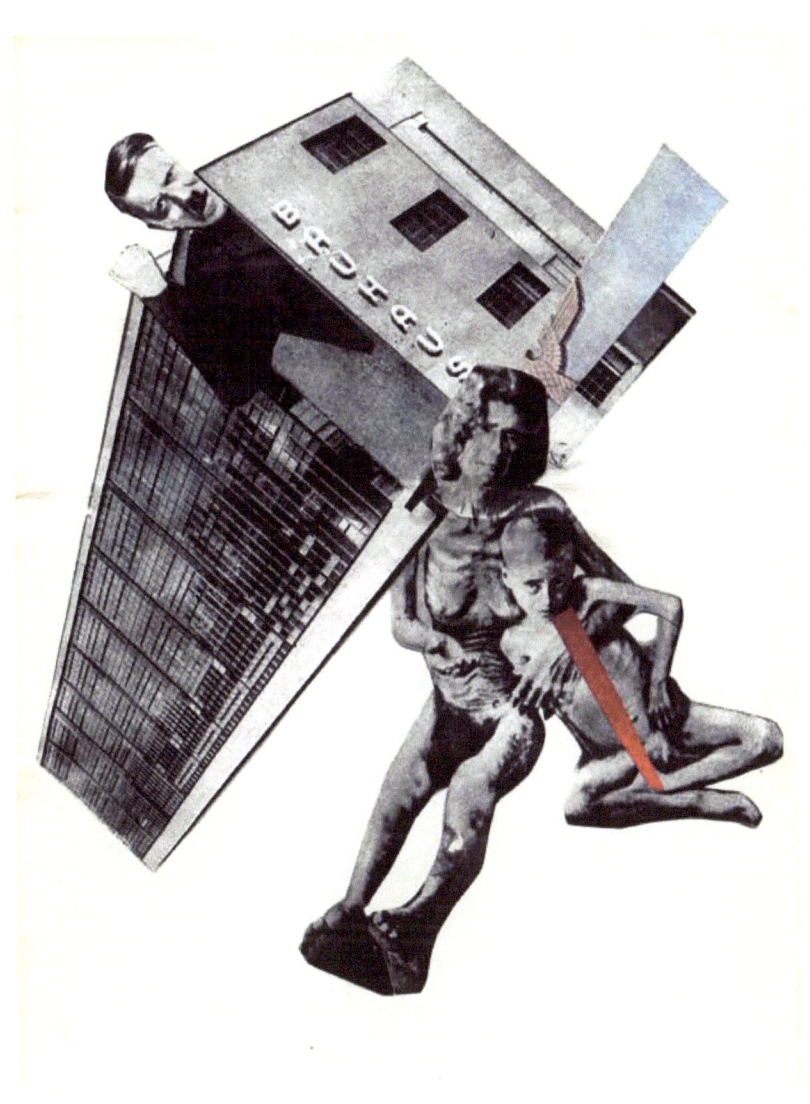

titeann nithe as a chéile . . .
tús an tséasúir
nua

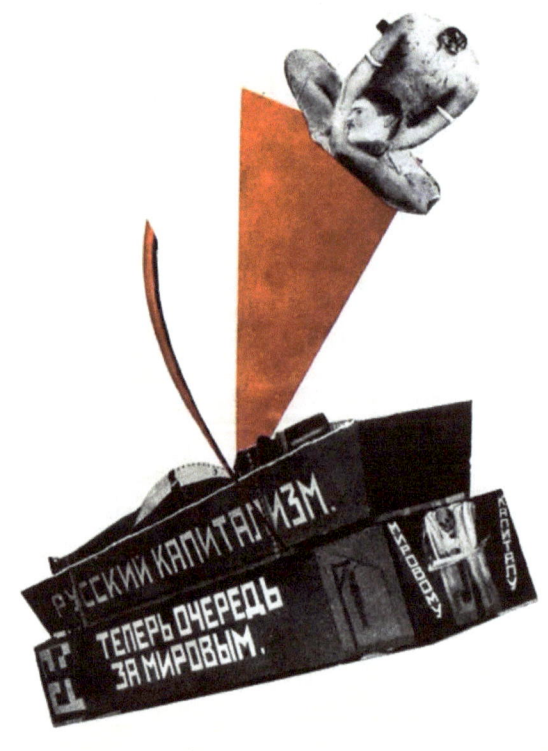

things fall apart . . .
a new season
begins

abair a dhuine chaoin
cén fhaid as seo
go dtí an sliabh beannaithe

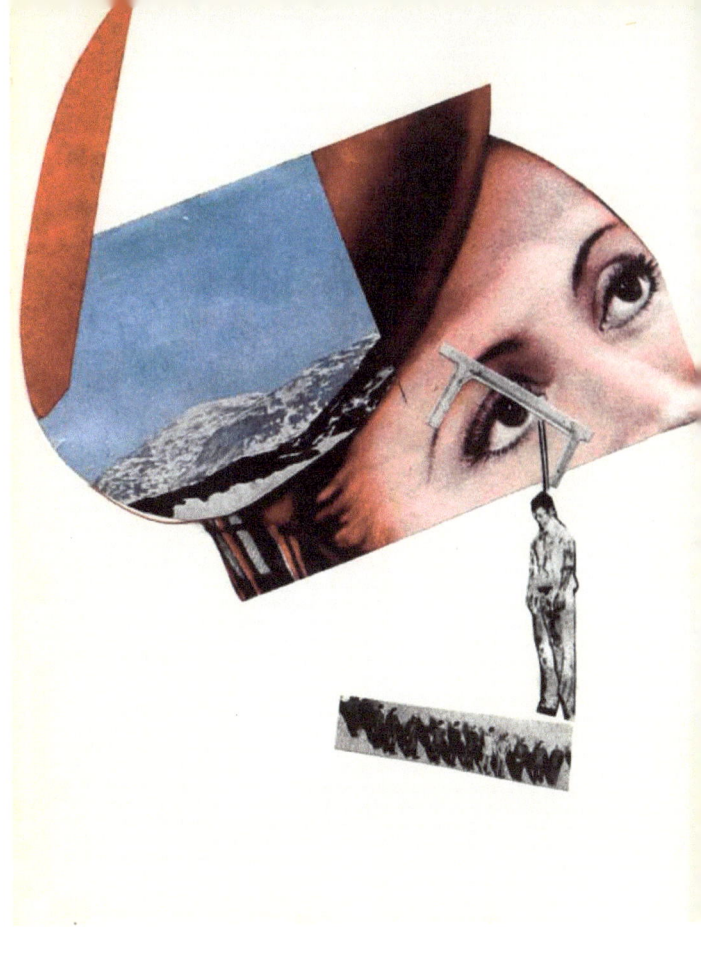

tell me kind sir
how far is it
to the sacred mountain

"The right art," cried the Master, "is purposeless, aimless! The more obstinately you try to learn how to shoot the arrow for the sake of hitting the goal, the less you will succeed in the one and the further the other will recede. What stands in your way is that you have a much too willful will. You think that what you do not do yourself does not happen."

Eugen Herrigel

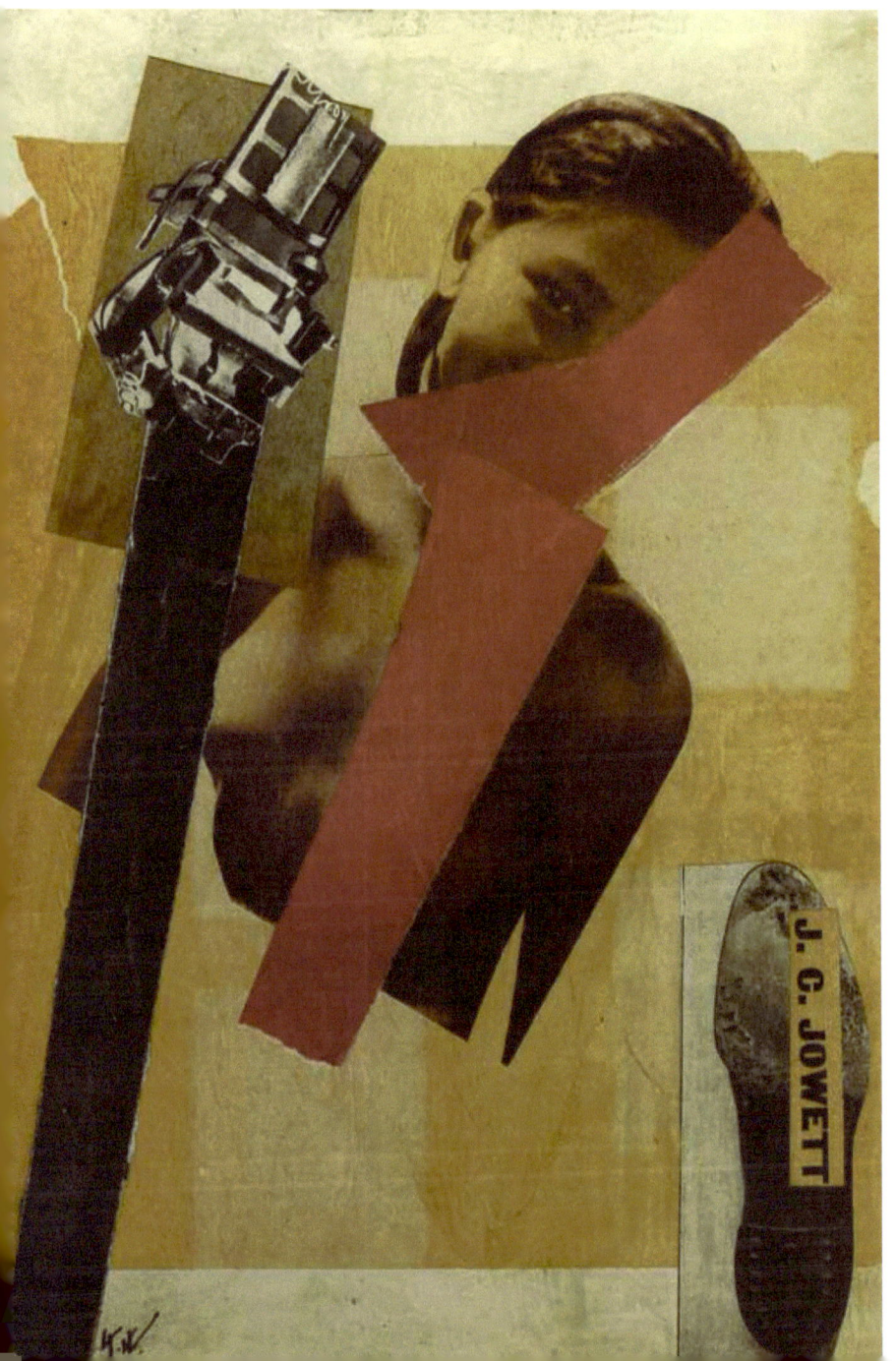

léi féin
i lár na hoíche—
cathaoir leictreach

alone
in the middle of the night—
electric chair

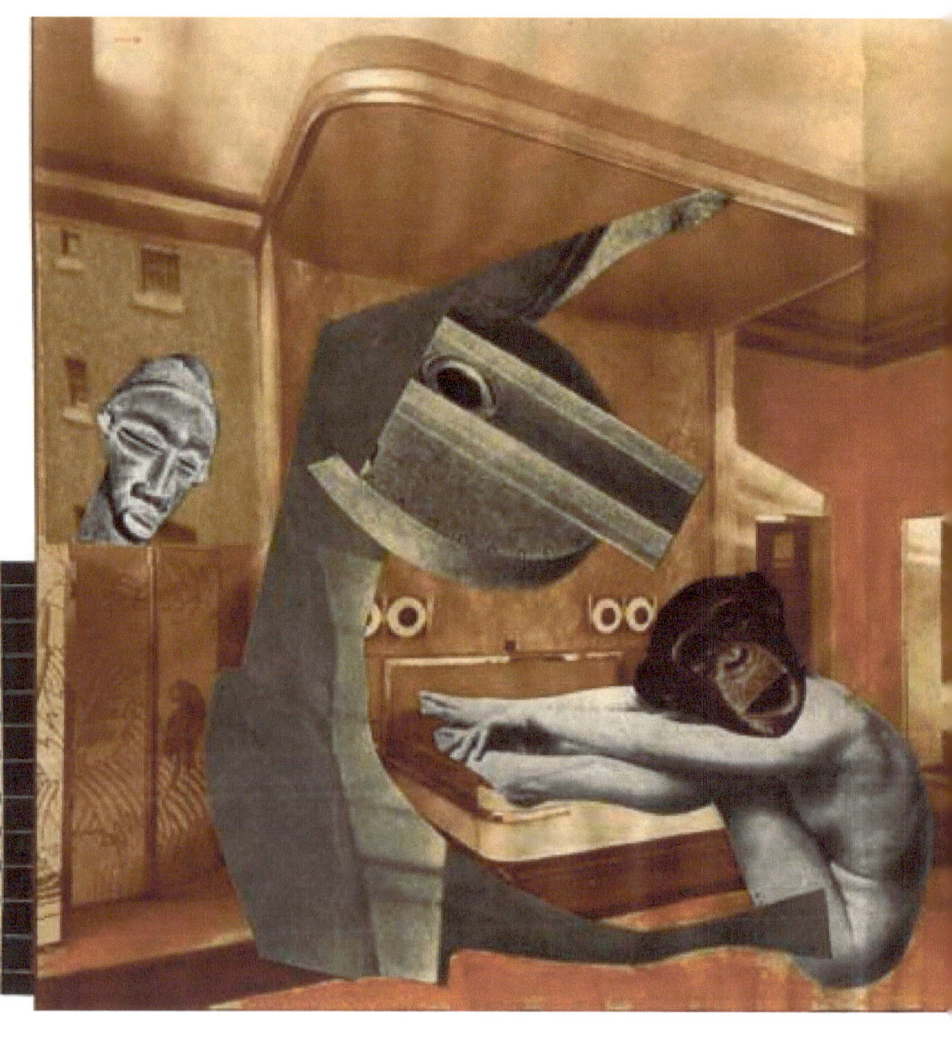

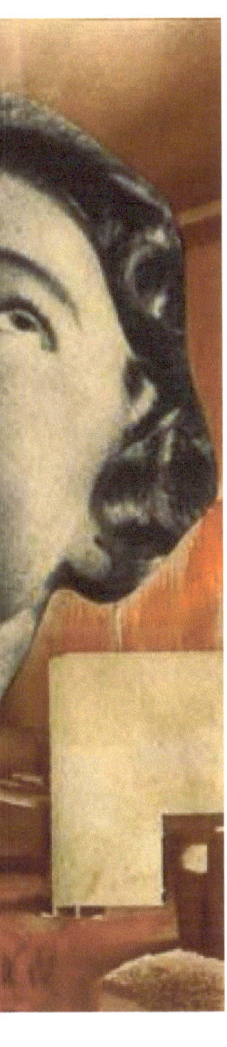

níl aon éalú—
an afraic ag féachaint isteach
an t-am ar fad

there's no escape—
africa looking in the window
all the time

an abhainn a d'fhág sí
agus na craobhaibhneacha—
ar a dearna

the river she left behind
and all its tributaries—
on her palm

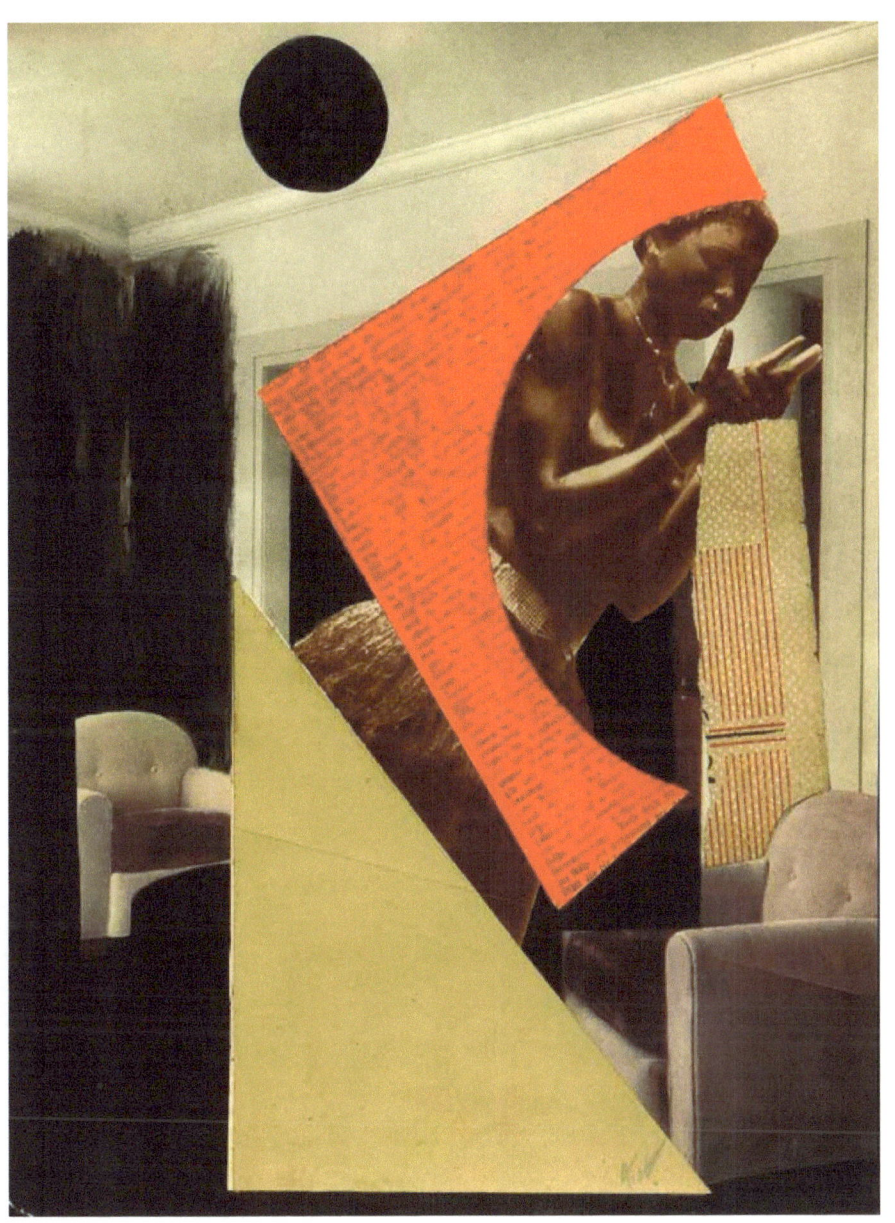

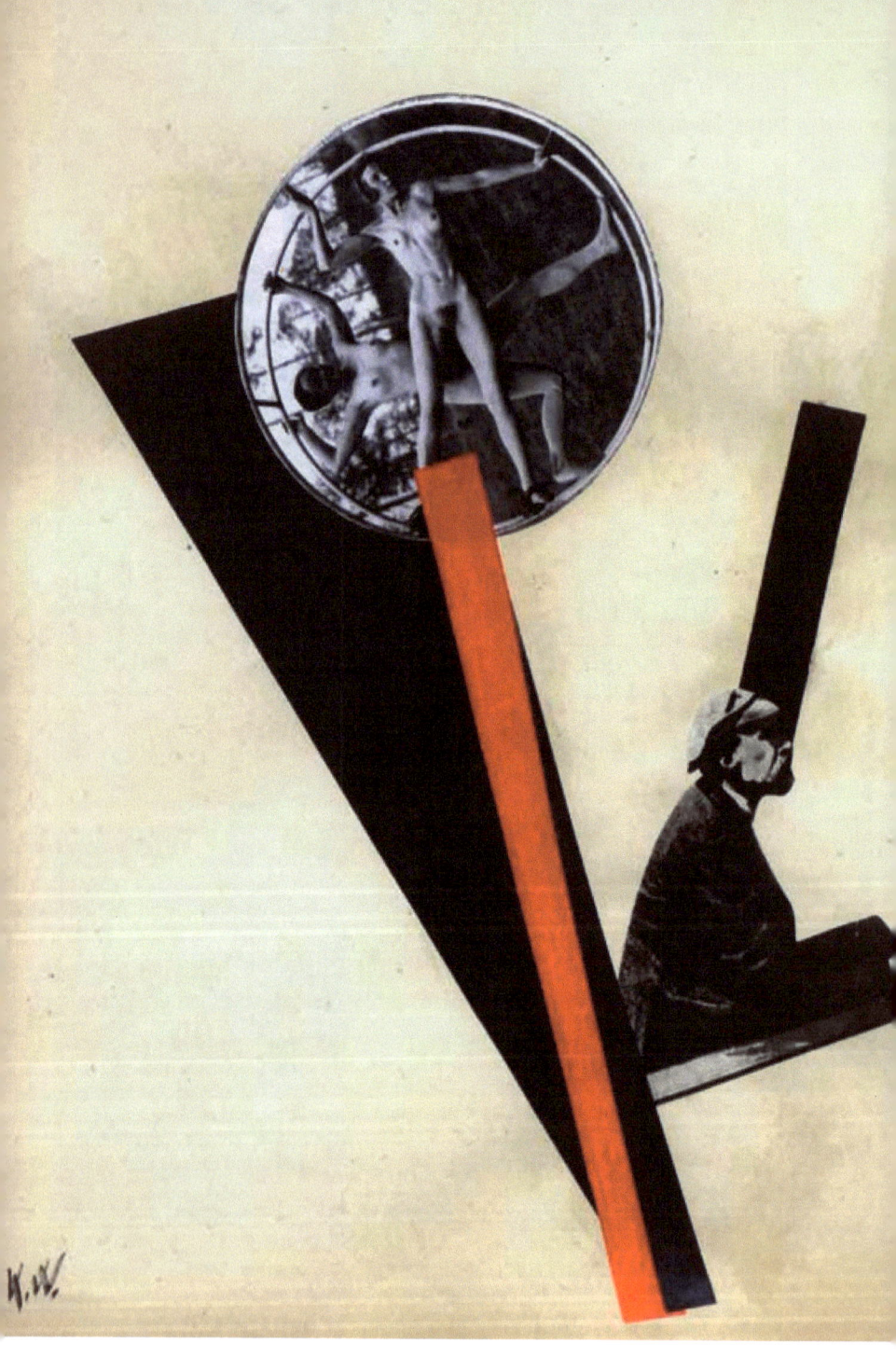

éist! an domhan
ag casadh is ag casadh
i gcónaí

listen! the world
still going round
and round and round

a dhuine chaoin
cá bhfaighinn teacht ar
an dochtúir loewe

kind sir
where can i find
doctor loewe

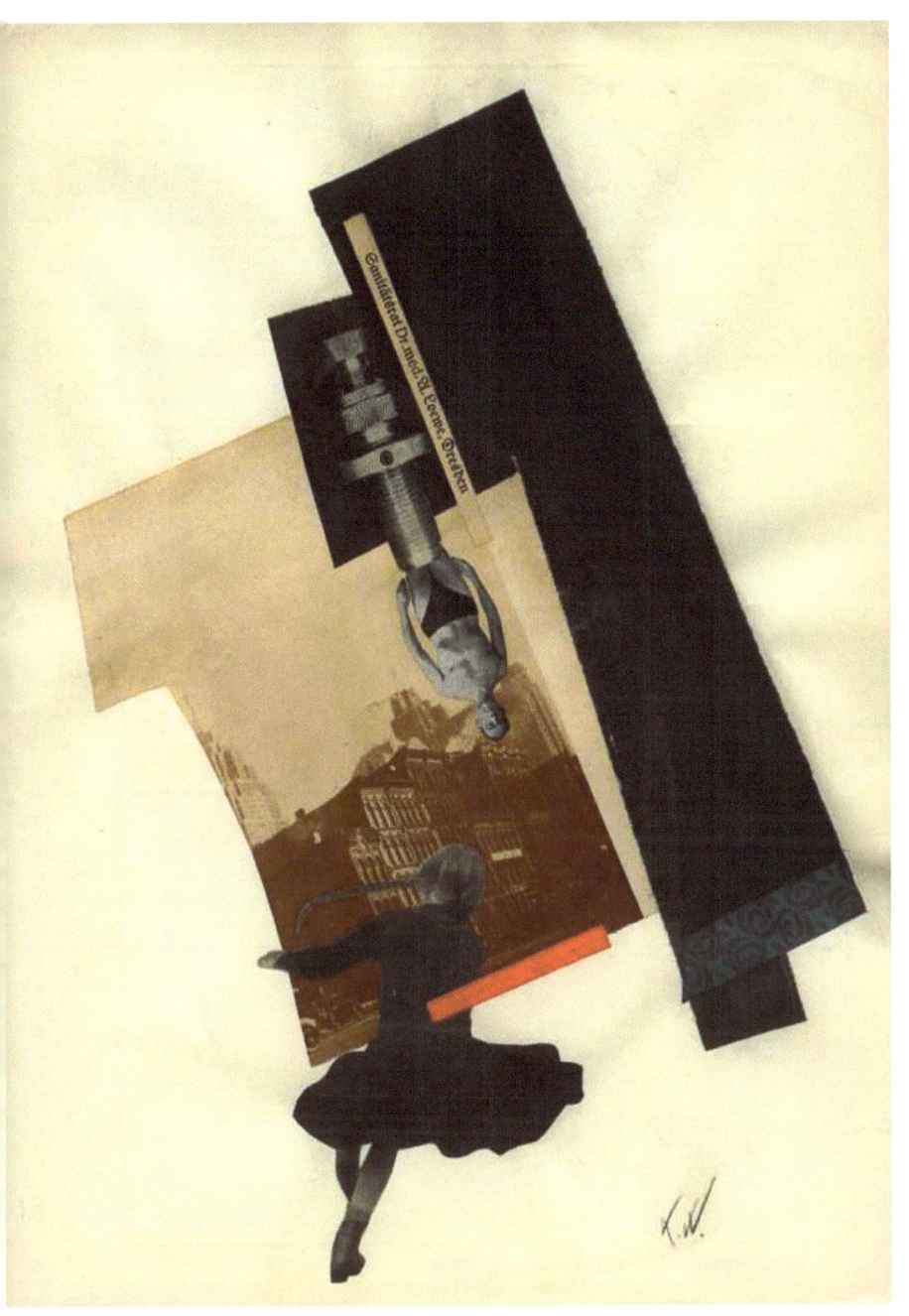

an chéad sioc—
adhmad á ghearradh
ag comharsa

first frost—
a neighbour chopping
firewood

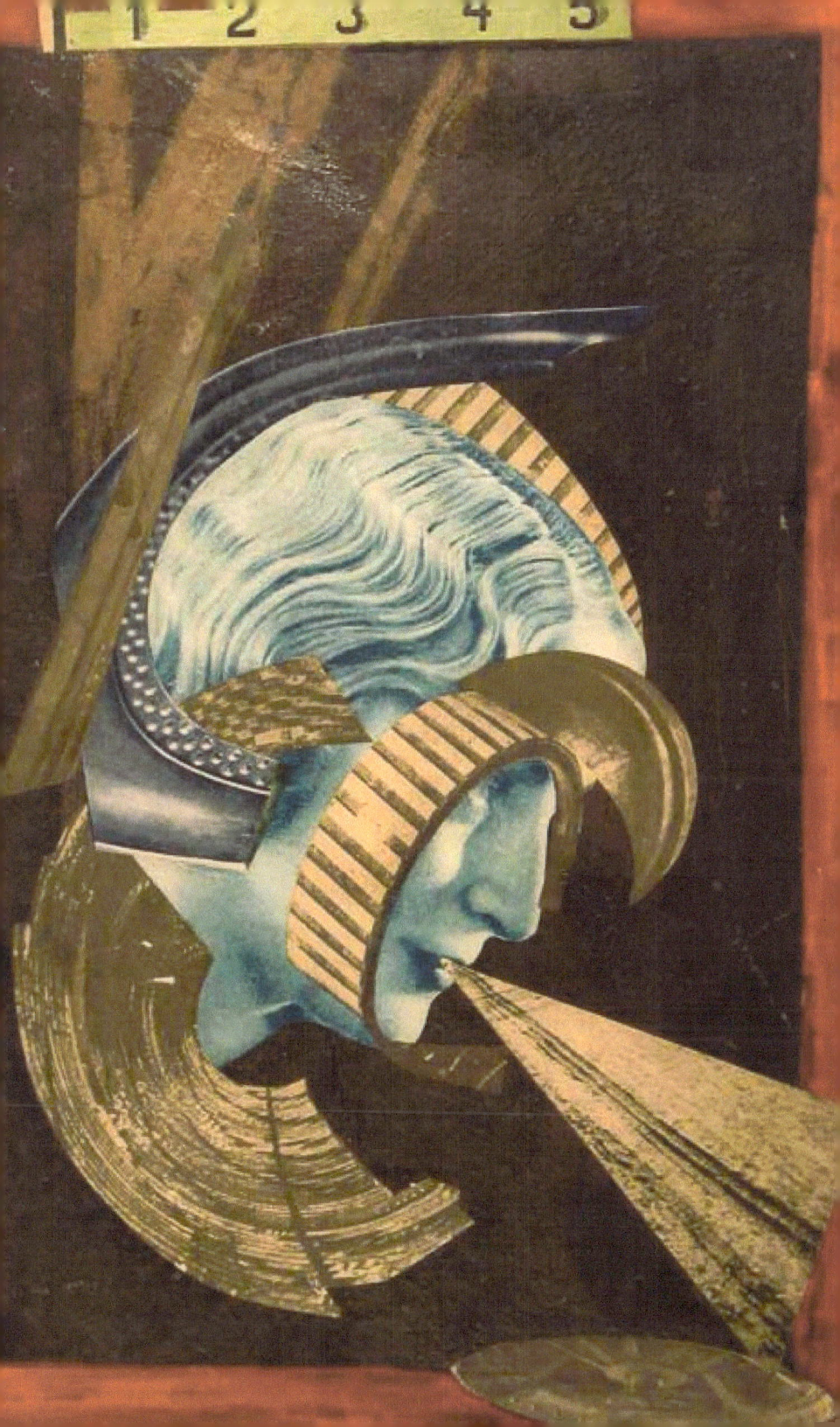

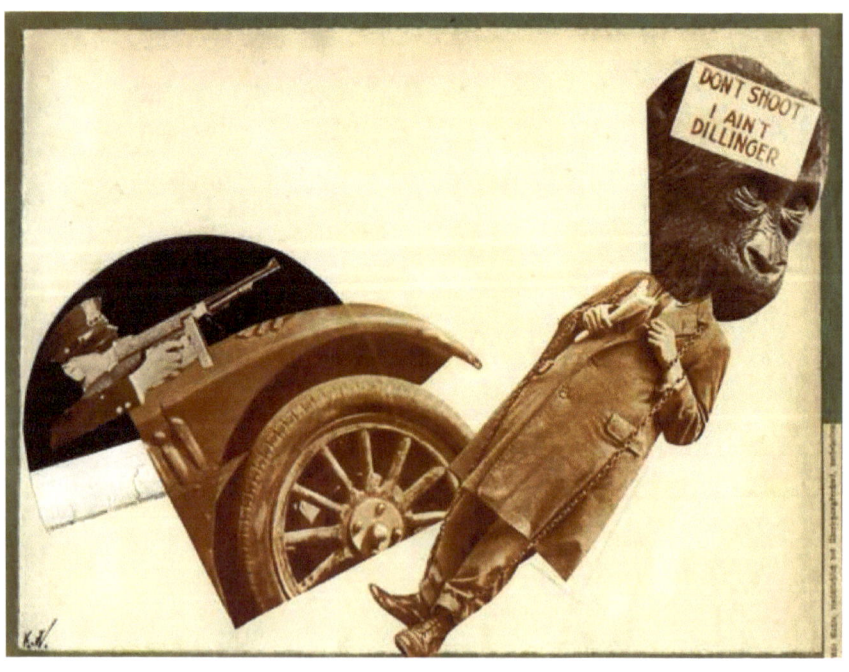

rinnfheitheamh géar:
is mé
dillinger

deep meditation:
i am
dillinger

"The hand that stretches the bow must open like a child's hand opens. What sometimes hinders the precision of the shot is the archer's over-active will. He thinks: 'What I fail to do will not be done', and that's not quite how things work. Man should always act, but he must also let other forces of the universe act in their own due time."

Eugen Herrigel

seanfhonn
dearúdta le fada—
deora reoite i ngloine vadca

an old
long-forgotten tune—
tears frozen in a glass of vodka

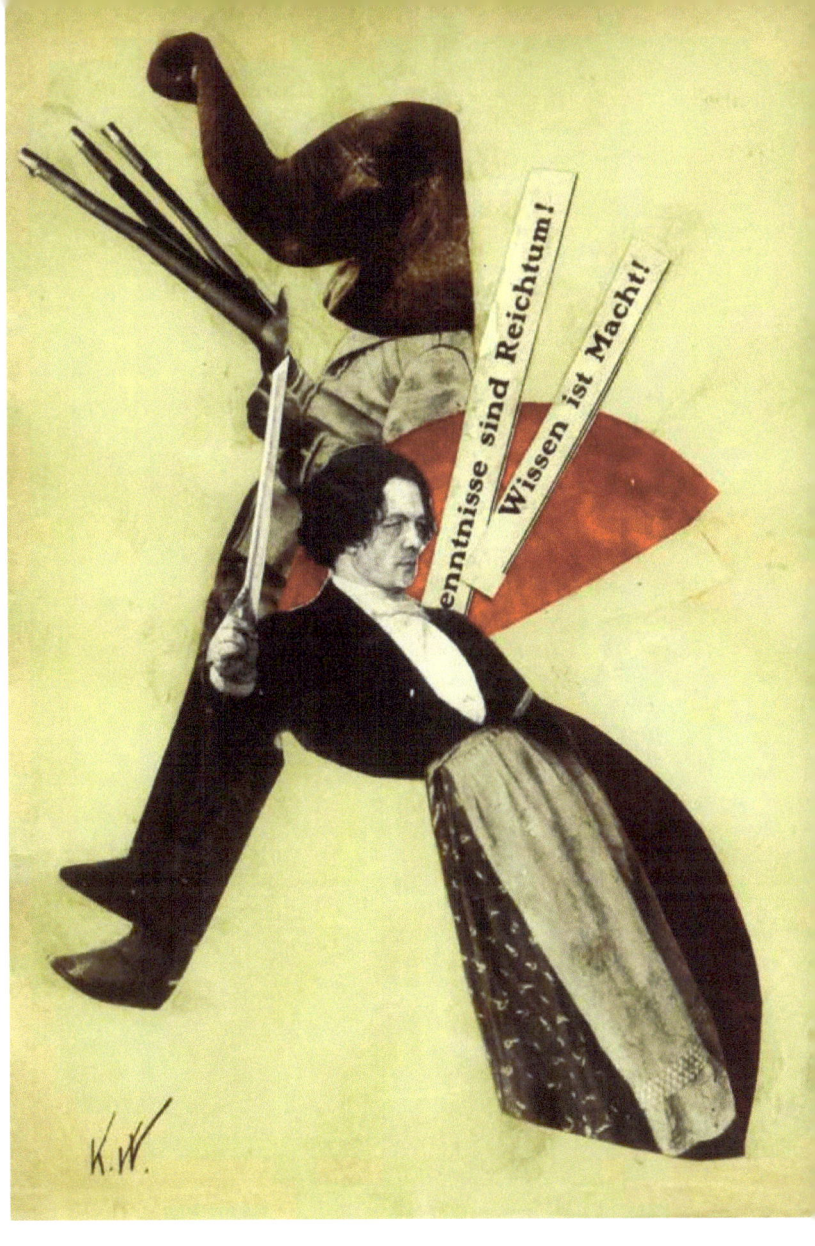

13

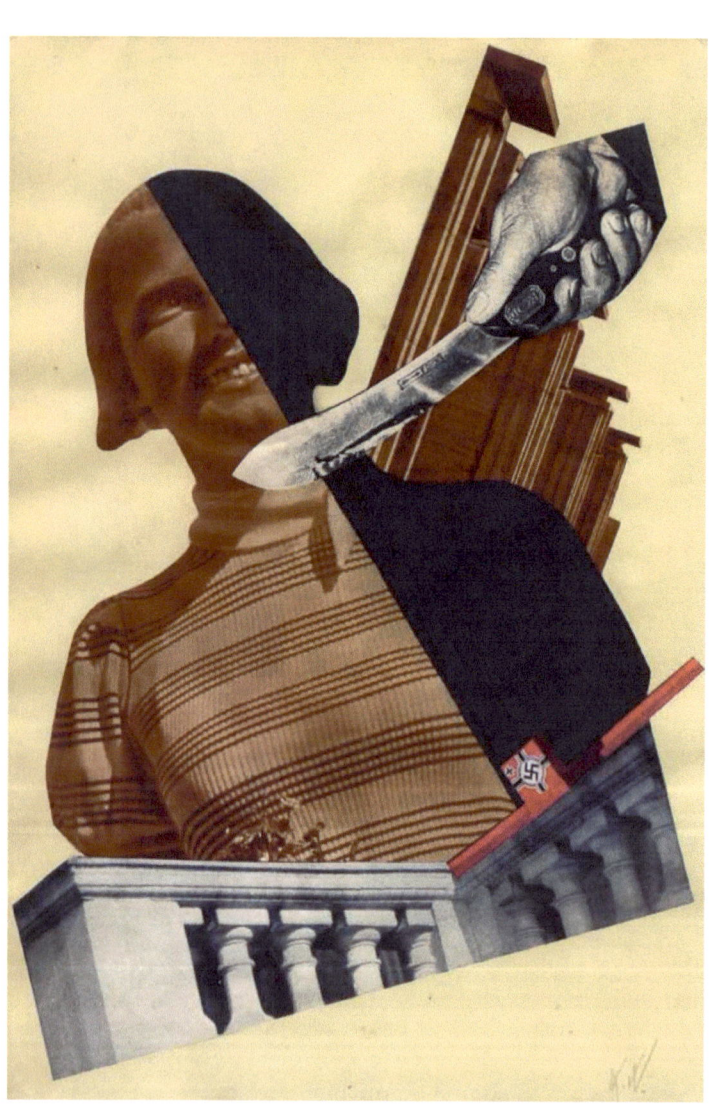

scian mhaith
scian an-mhaith
f.dick

it is a good knife
a very good knife
f.dick

14

rinnfheitheamh maidine . . .
snag easa
i gcéin

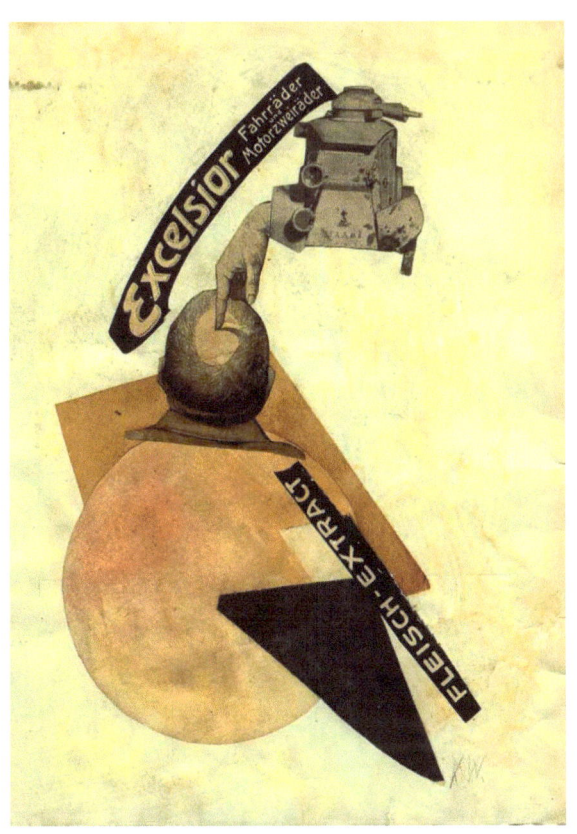

morning meditation . . .
the distant sob
of a waterfall

the giraffe
is not the answer—
world hunger

ní réiteach na faidhbe
é an sioráf—
ocras domhanda

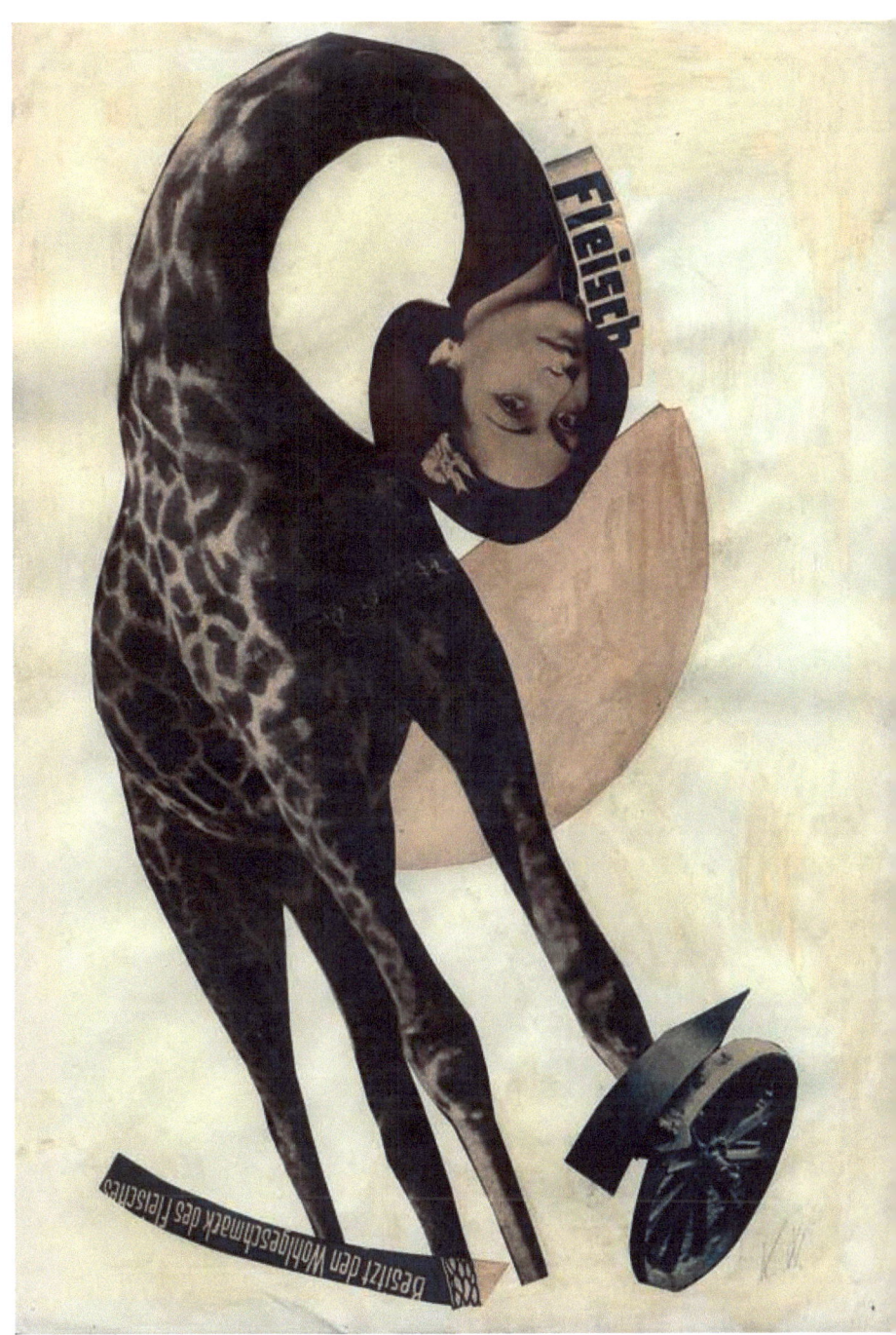

Fleisch

Besitzt den Wohlgeschmack des Fleisches

16

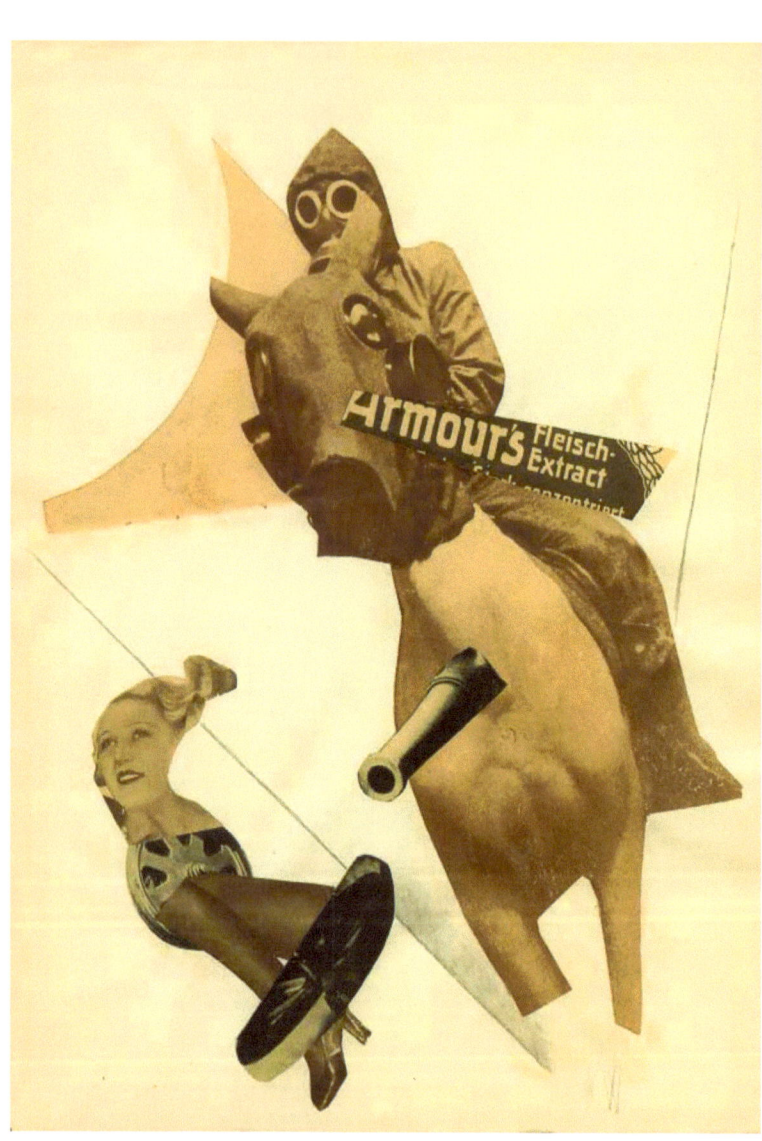

kind sir
where can i find
the dalai lama

a dhuine chaoin
cá bhfaighinn teacht
ar an dalaí láma

the girls who laughed
and cried with us—
geese flying north

na cailíní a gháir linn
is a chaoin—
géanna ag eitilt ó thuaidh

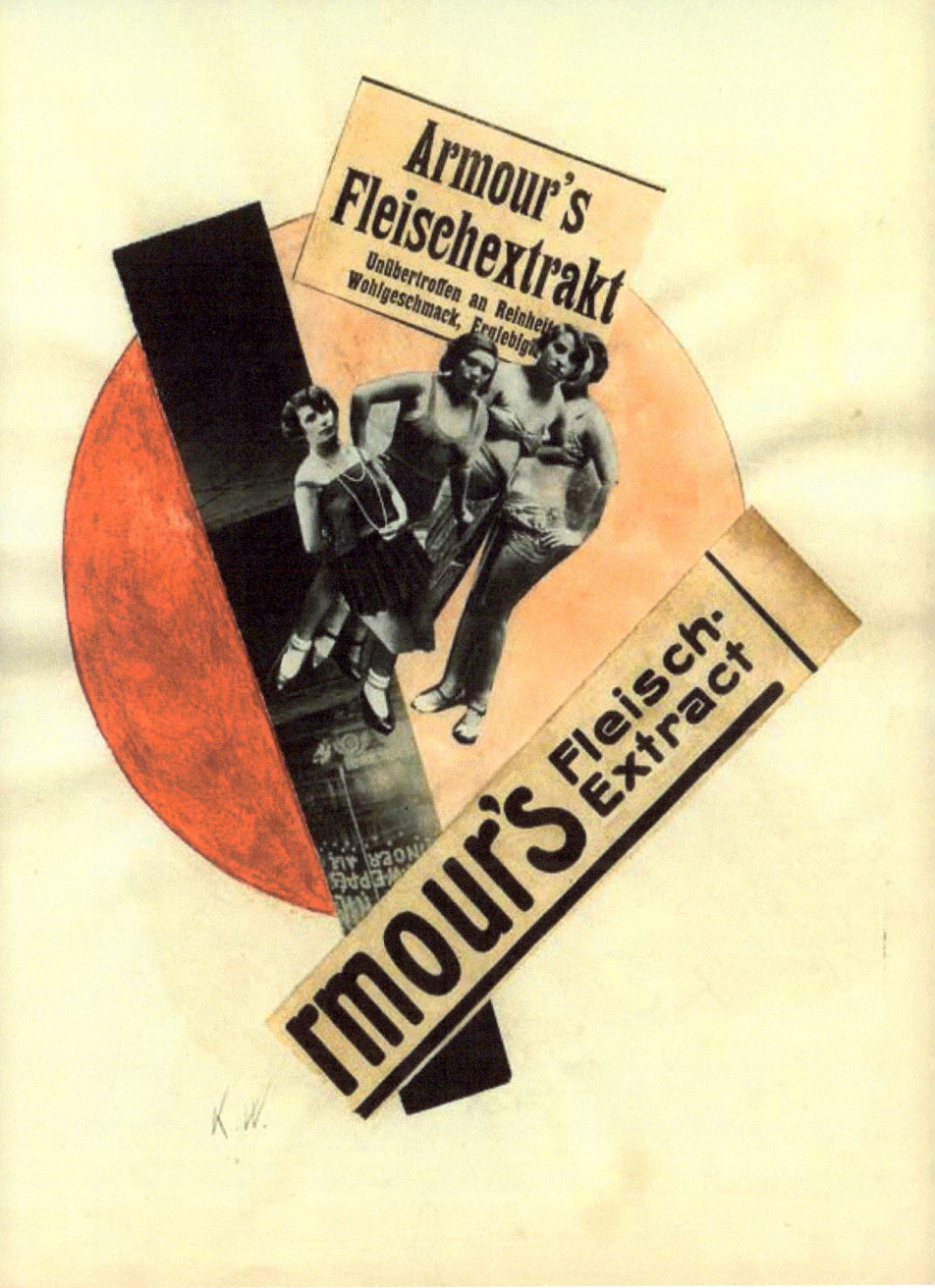

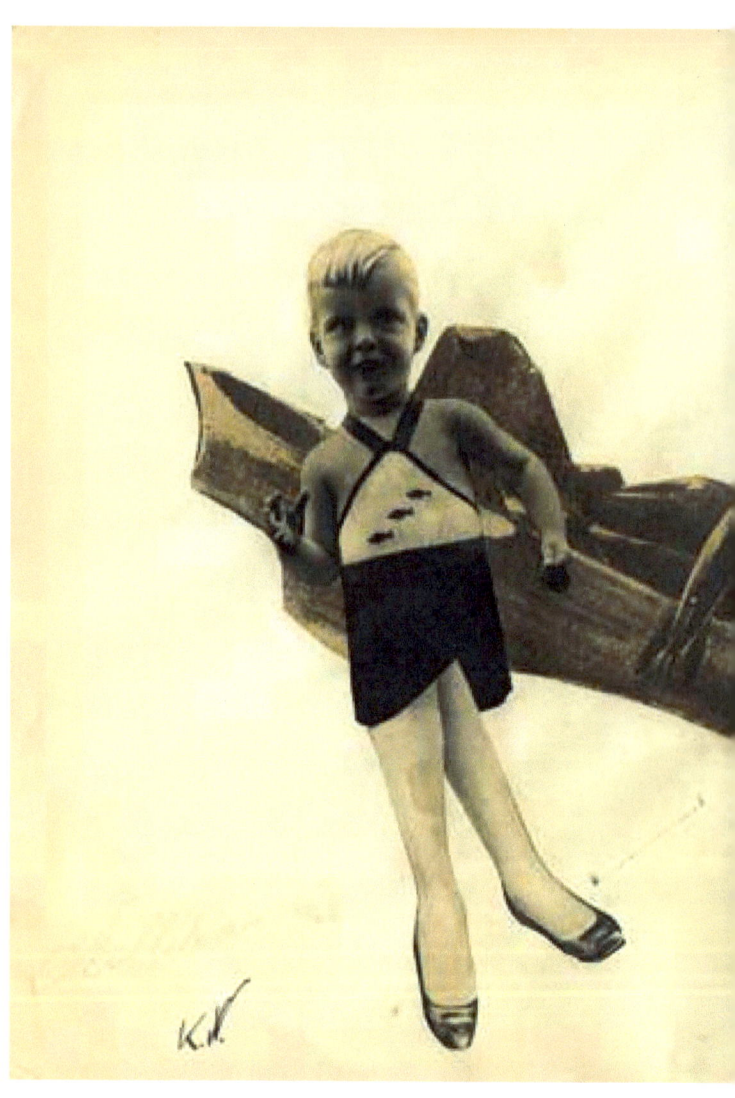

a dhuine chaoin
táim ar strae ní foláir—
tús an fhómhair

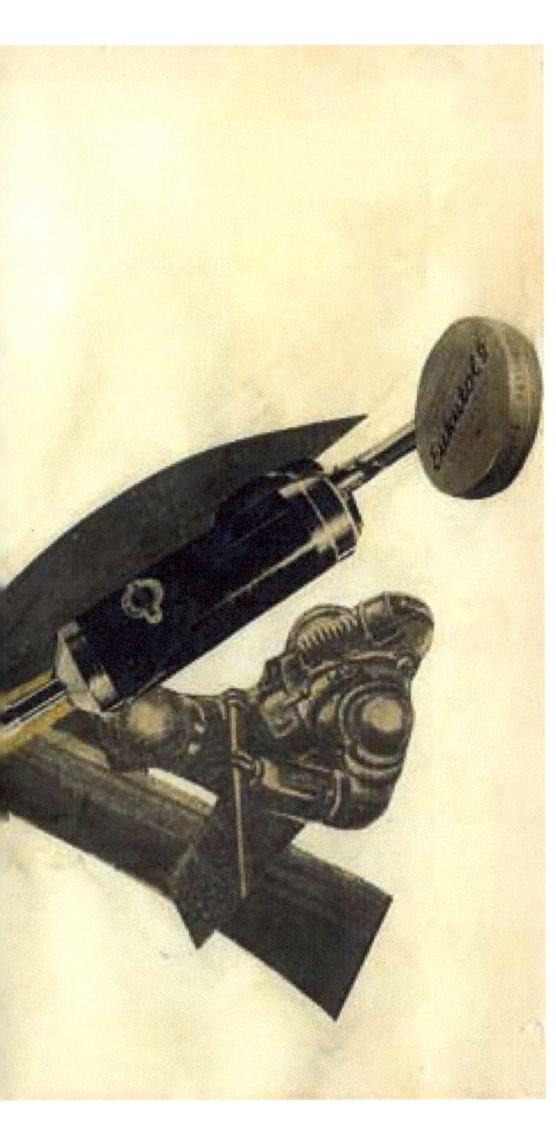

kind sir
i seem to be lost—
first days of autumn

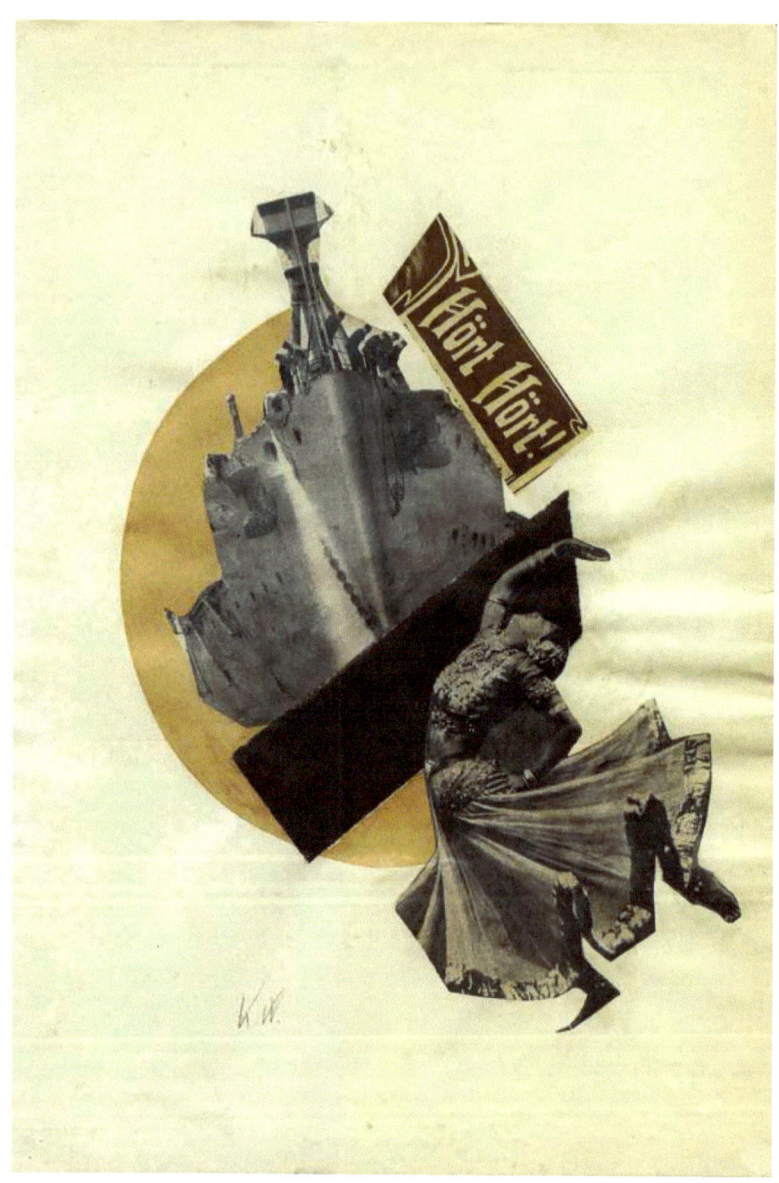

rincimis
mar nár rinceamar riamh cheana—
tá na mairnéalaigh chugainn

let us dance
like we've never danced before—
the sailors are here!

duilleoga le gaoth . . .
buaileann an guthán
is stadann

leaves scatter in the wind . . .
the phone rings
and stops

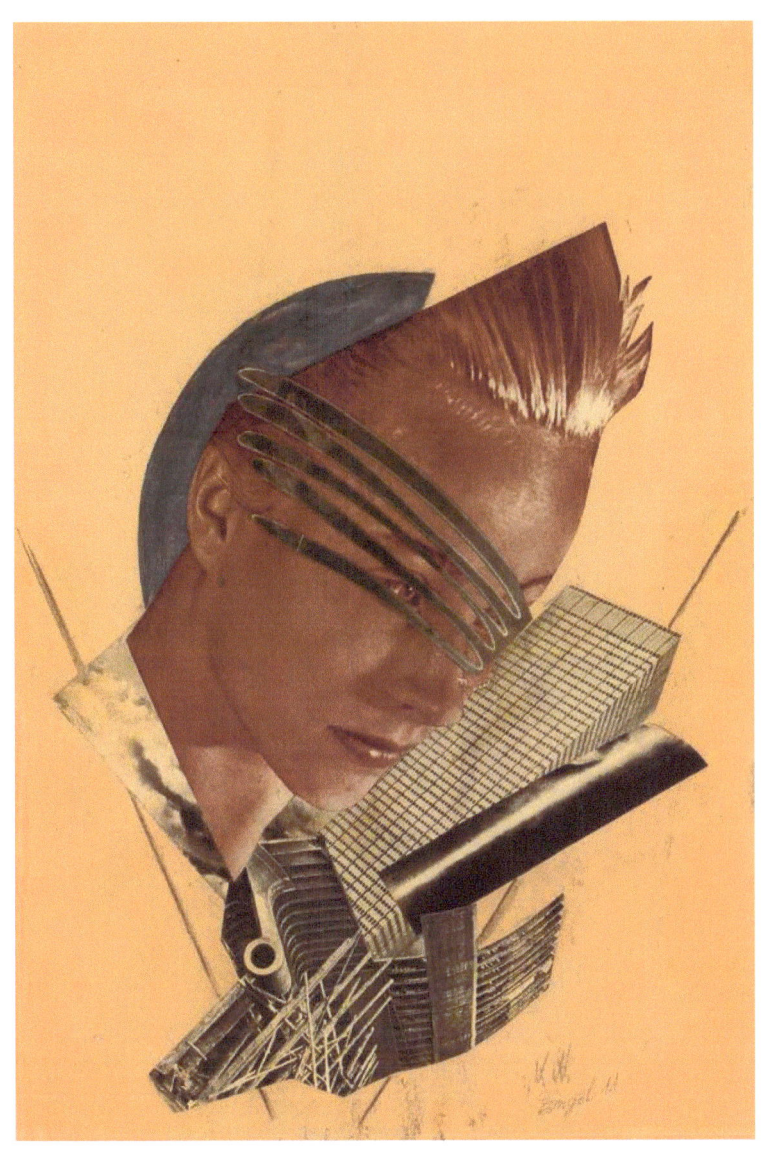

21

titeann an crogall ina chodladh . . .
ní baol níos mó
do na réaltaí

a crocodile falls asleep . . .
it's safe now
for stars to emerge

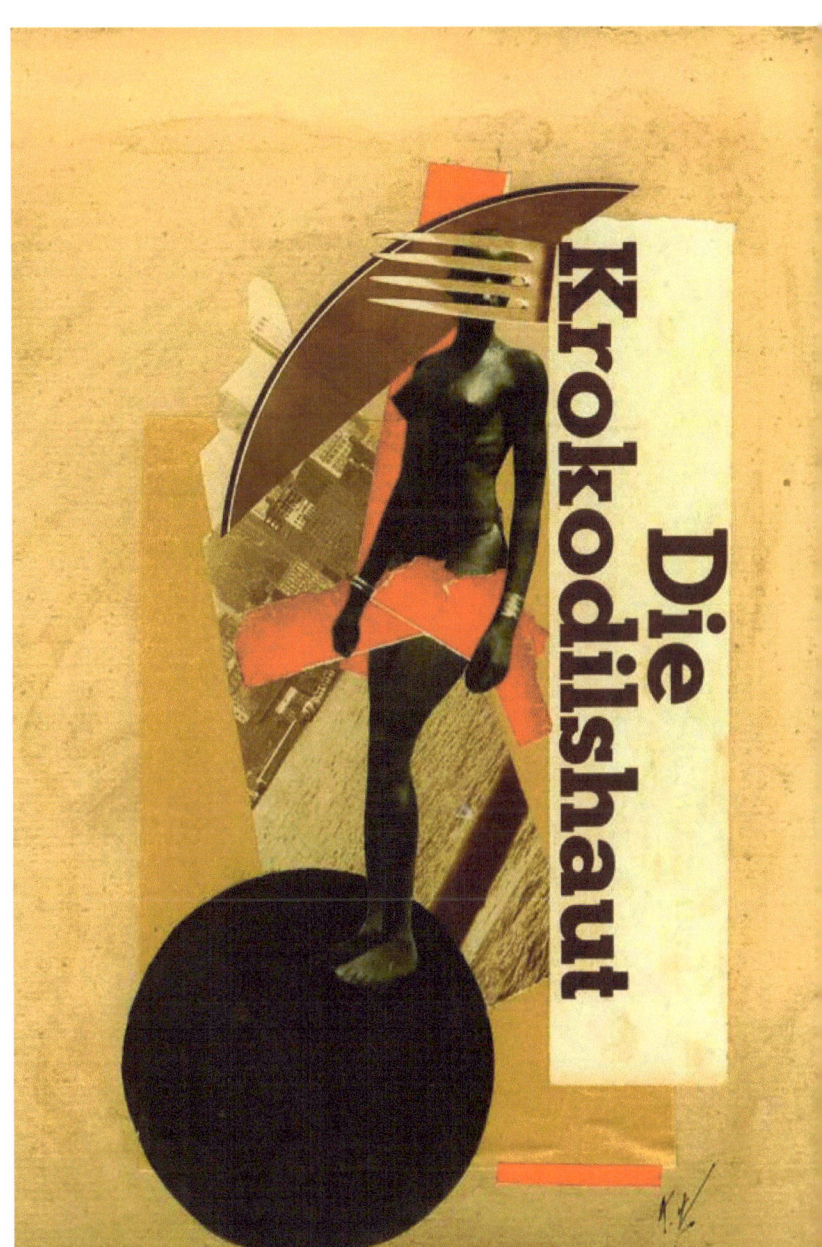

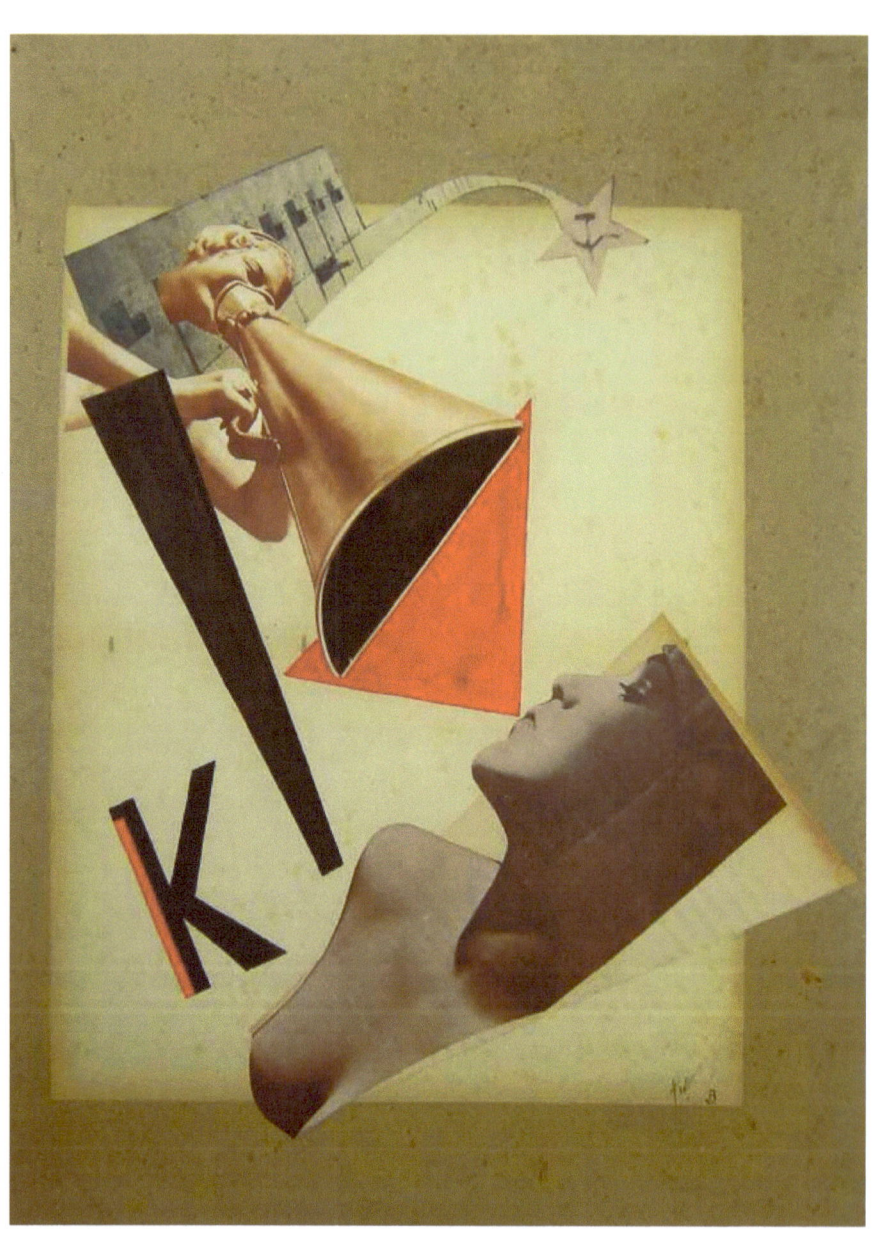

brollach chléópátra—
an taibhreamh céanna arís
ag an nathair

cleopatra's breast—
the recurring dream
of a poisonous snake

labhrann préachán ó chraobh:
d'fhéadadh sé tosnú arís . . .
an gealtachas

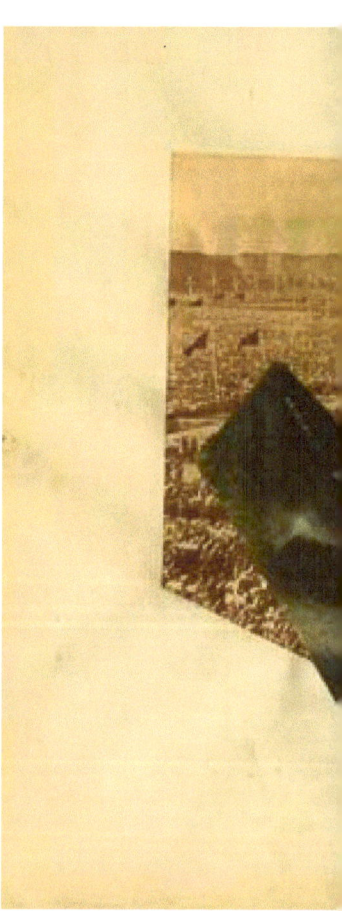

a crow speaks from a branch:
it could start all over again . . .
the madness

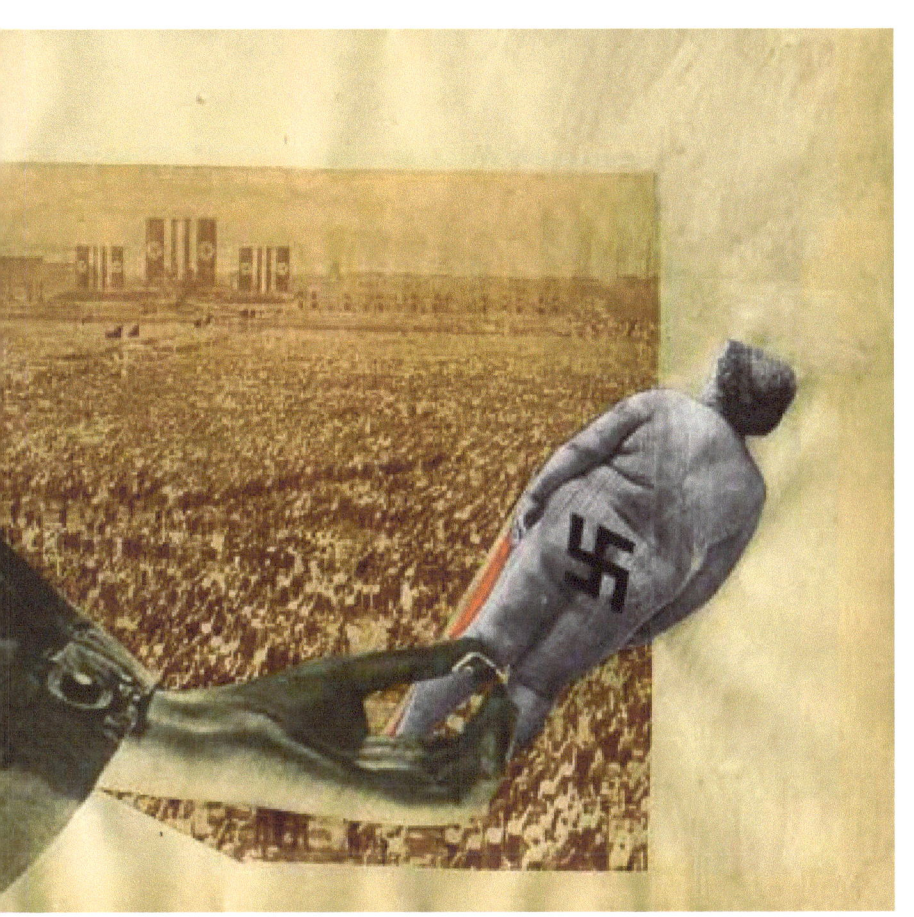

a dhuine chaoin
le do thoil
an san arcáid atáim

kind sir
pray tell me
is this arcadia

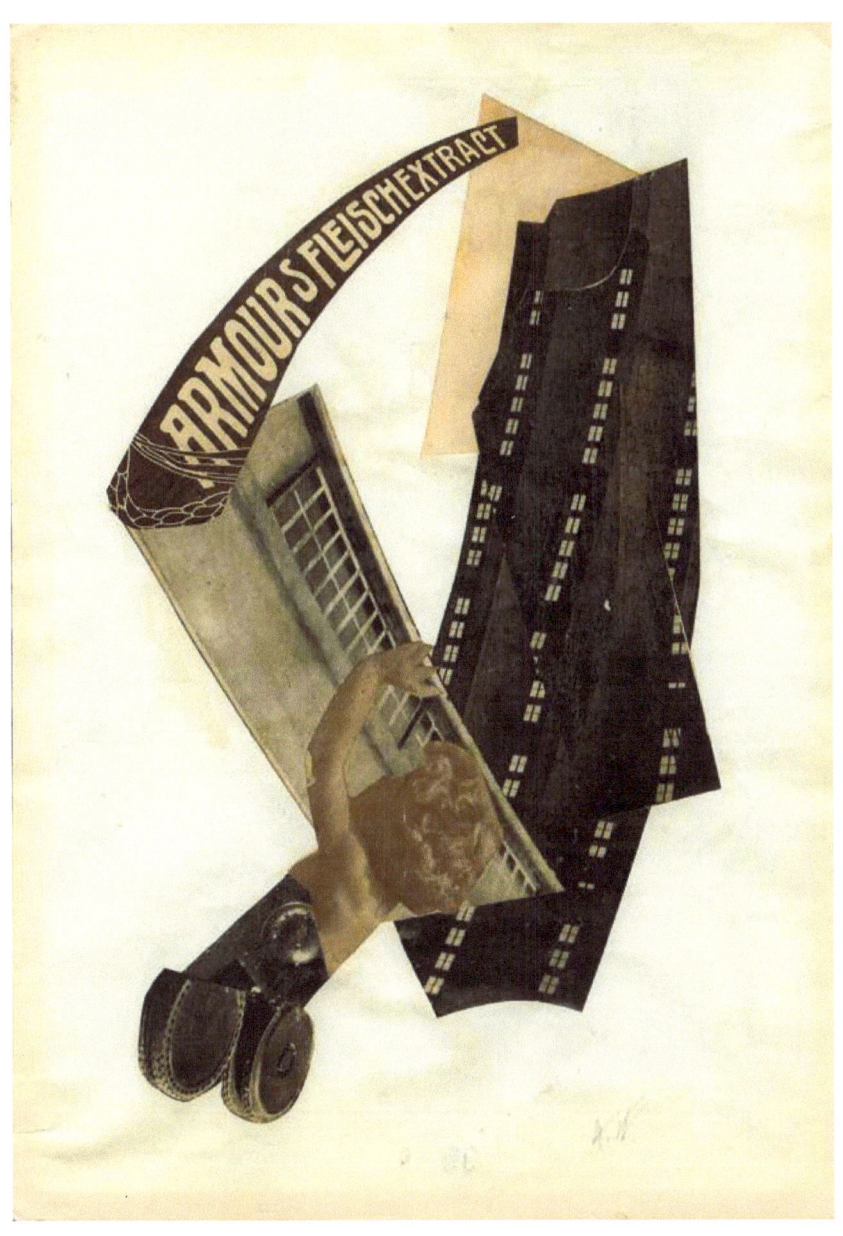

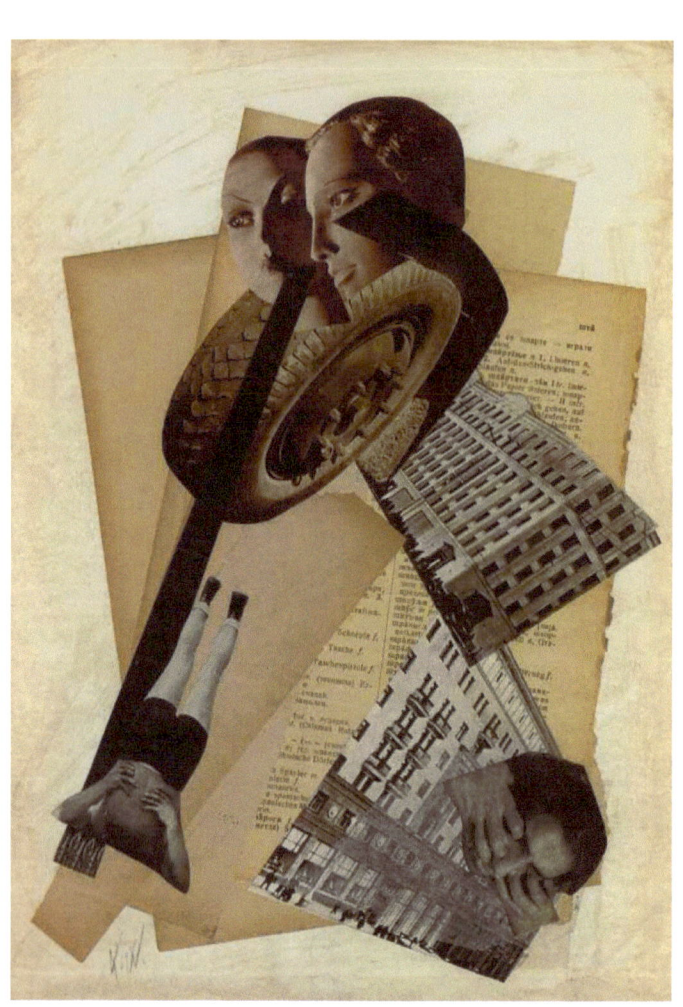

spring morning . . .
one by one
words are perishing

maidin earraigh . . .
ina gceann is ina gceann
briathra ag éag

old folks' home—
a war veteran remembers the
taste of mother's milk

áras seandaoine—
is cuimhin le seansaighdiúir blas
bhainne a mháthar

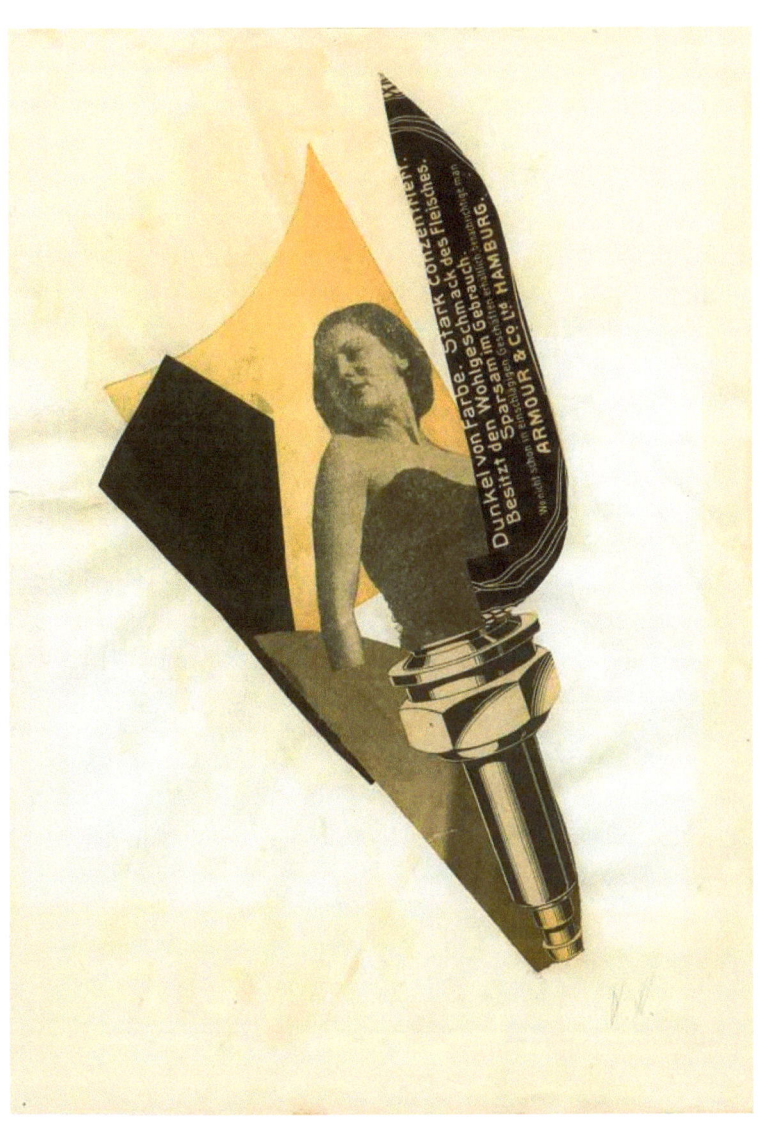

"This means that the mind or spirit is present anywhere, because it is nowhere attached to any particular place. And it can remain present because, even when related to this or that object, it does not cling to it by reflection and thus lose its original mobility."

Eugen Herrigel

gort órga—
siamsa drúchta
sa dias chruithneachta

field of gold—
symphony of dew
in an ear of wheat

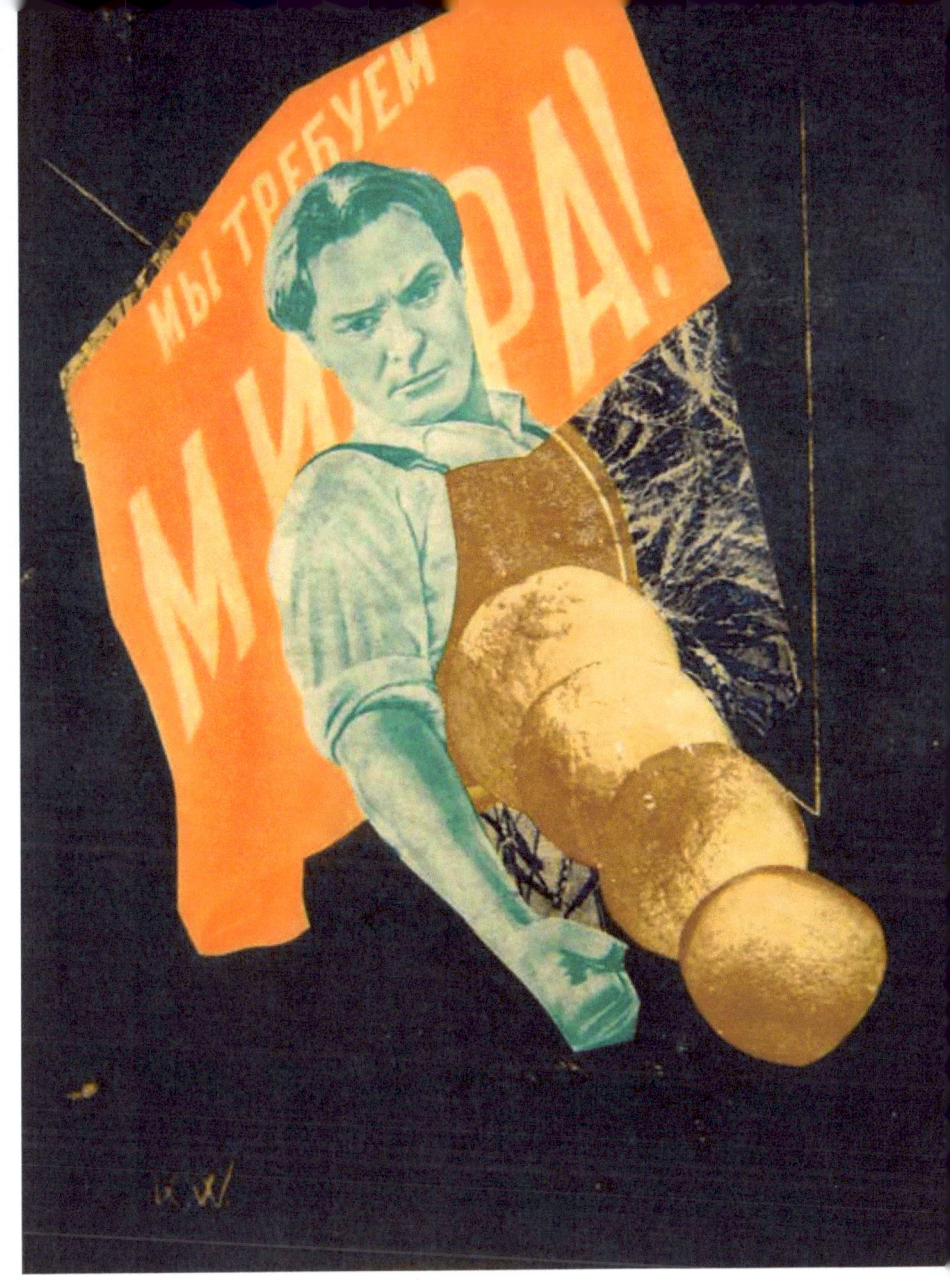

28

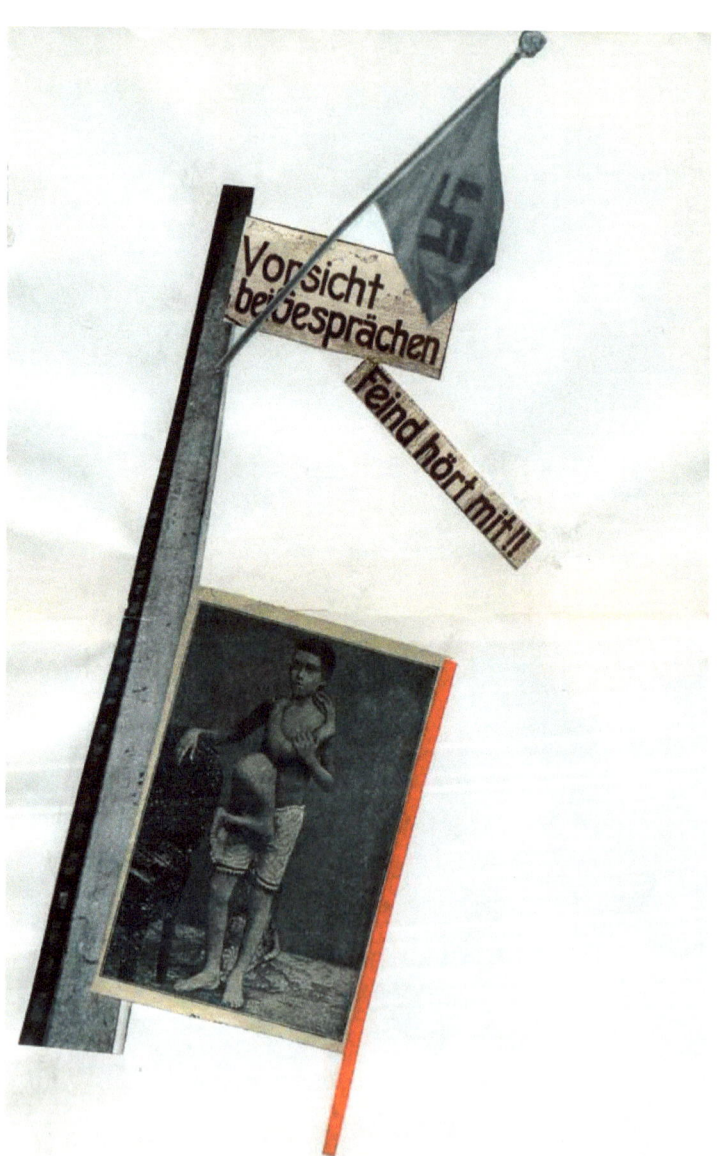

blátha silíní—
borradh iontach
faoi thionscal na háilleachta

cherry blossoms
how wonderfully it grows—
the beauty industry

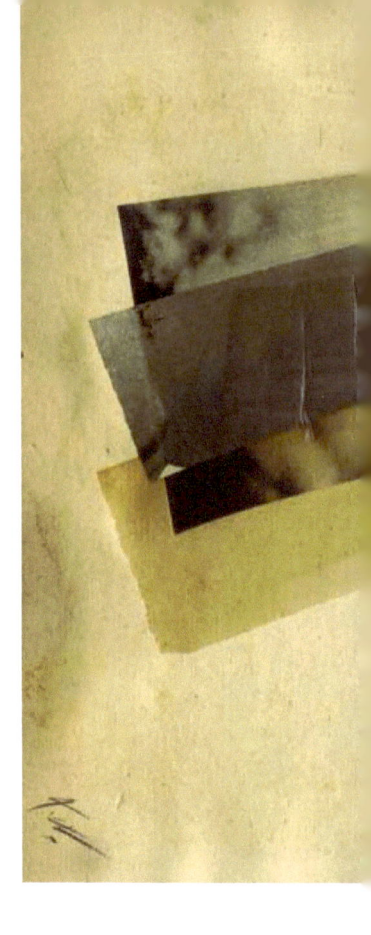

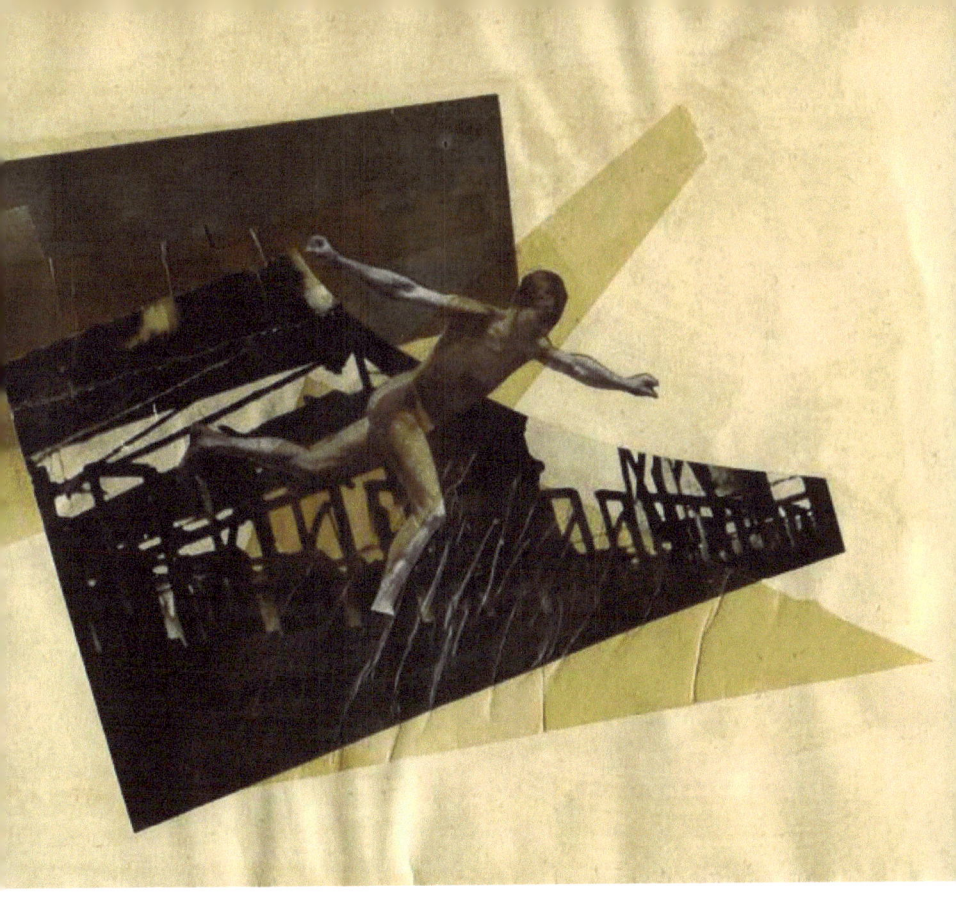

trying
to outrun himself—
an athlete

ag iarraidh
é féin a shárú—
lúthchleasaí

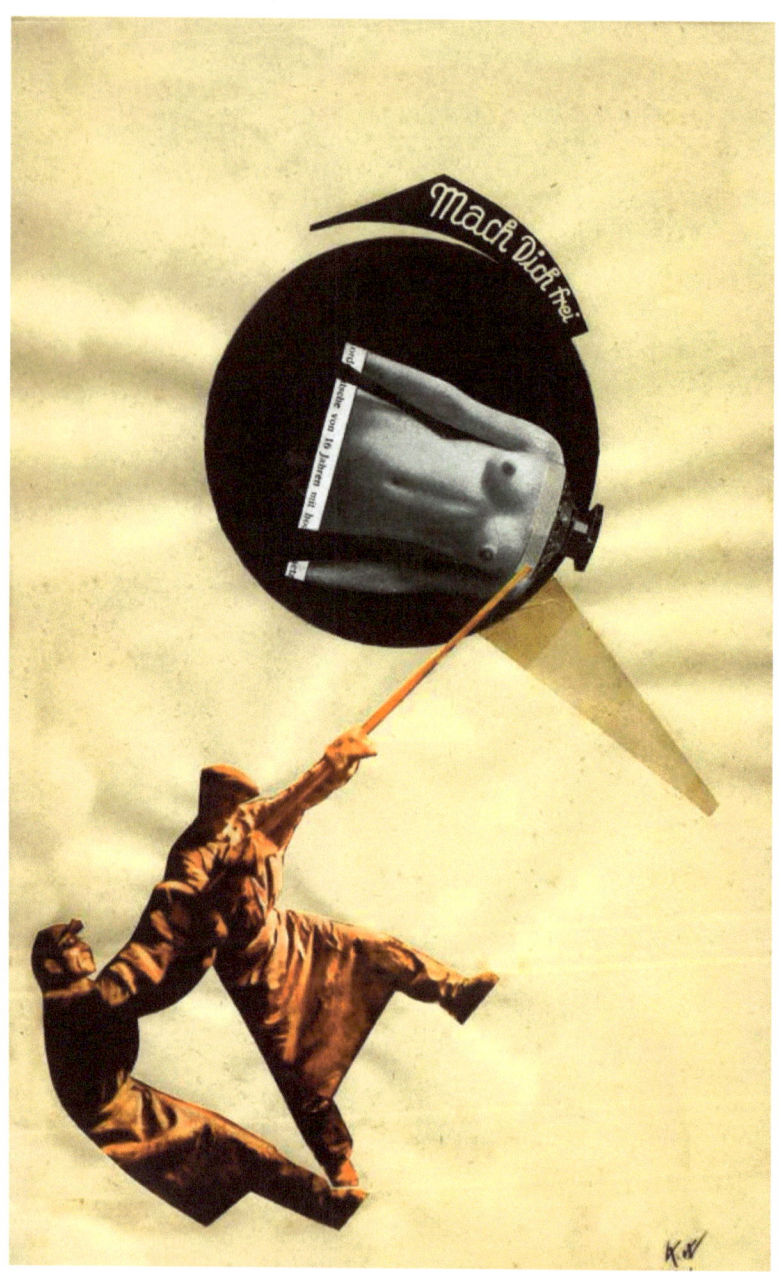

seanlochán
léimeann cailín nocht ann—
a chríoch

old pond
a naked girl jumps in—
the end

zen in ealaín
an naitsíochais—
eugen herrigel?!

zen in the art
of nazism—
eugen herrigel!?

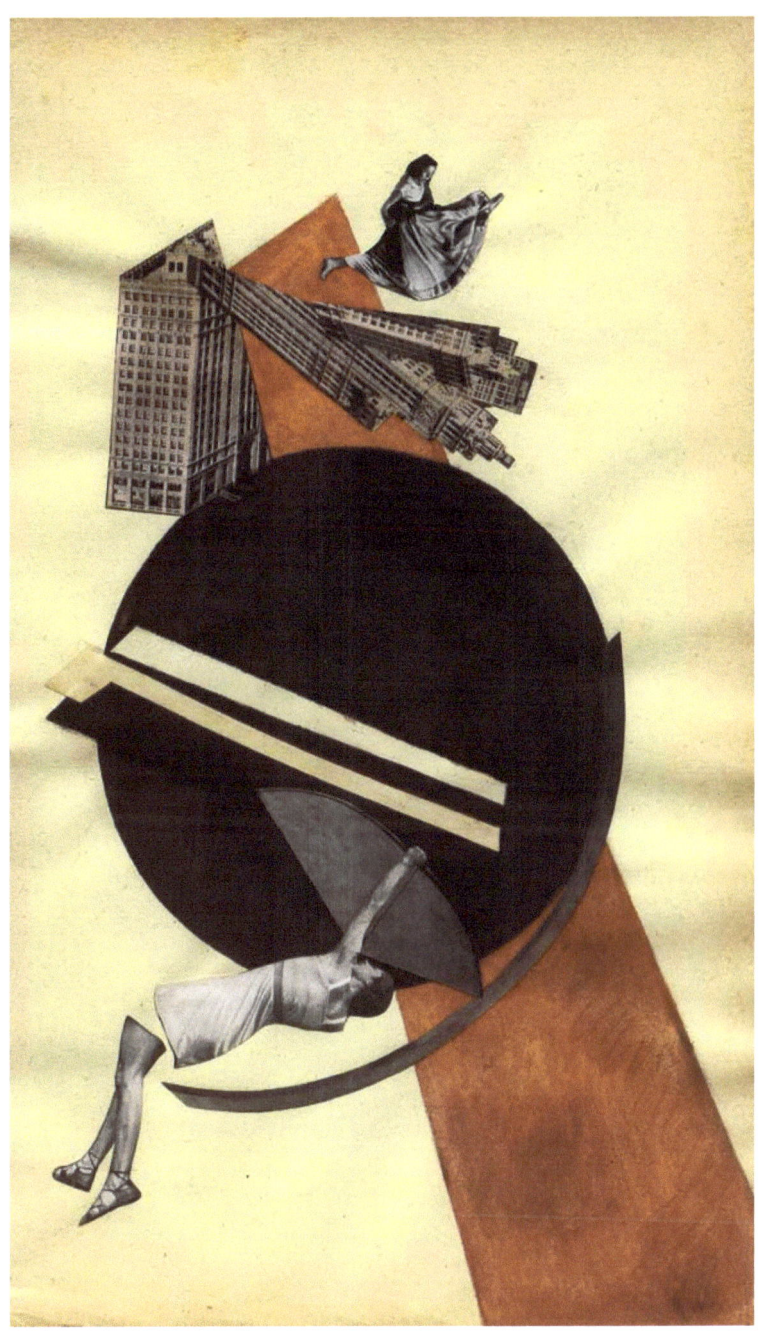

toirneach i gcéin—
neadaithe inár ndúchas
san afraic

thunder in the distance—
nestling in our african
origins

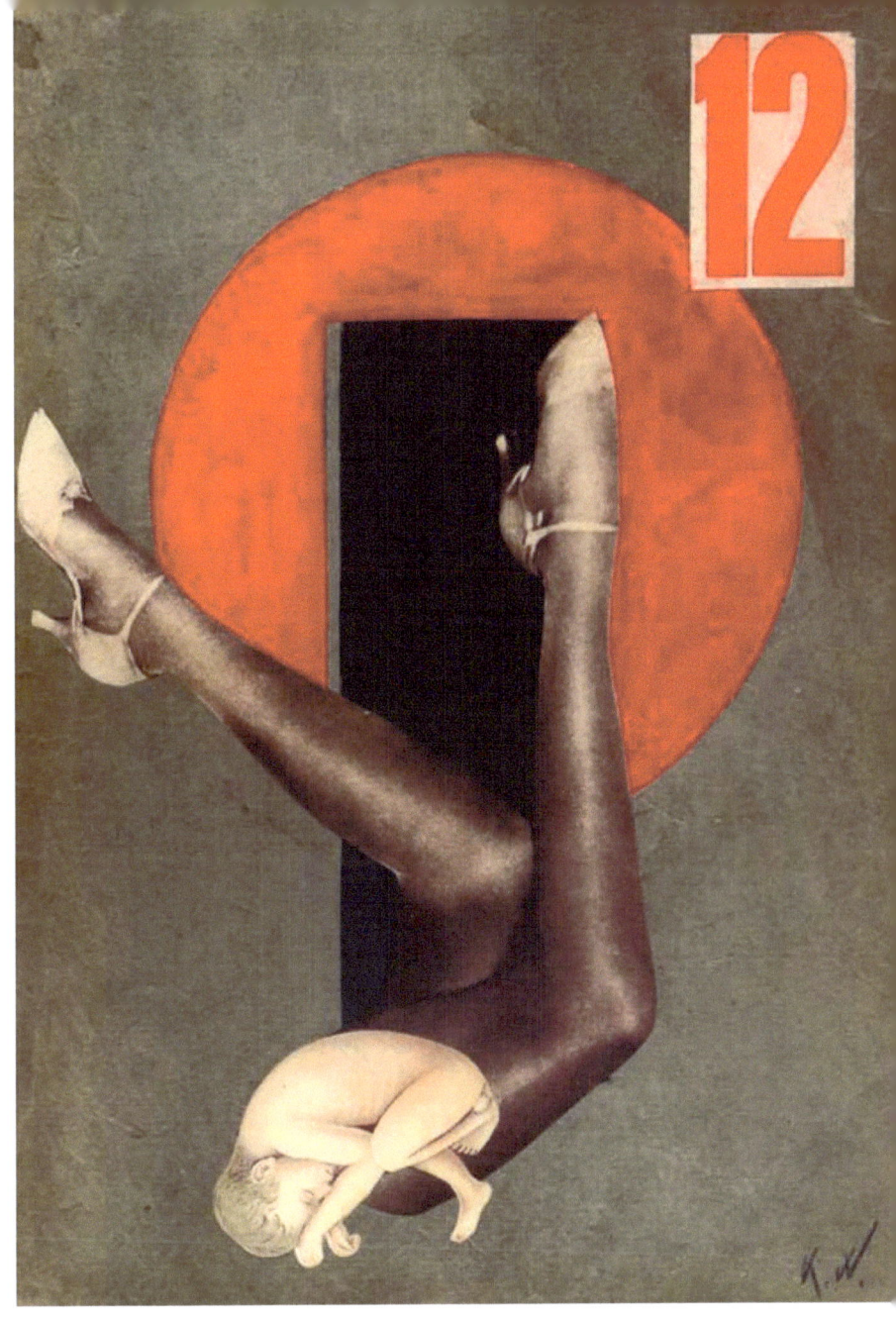

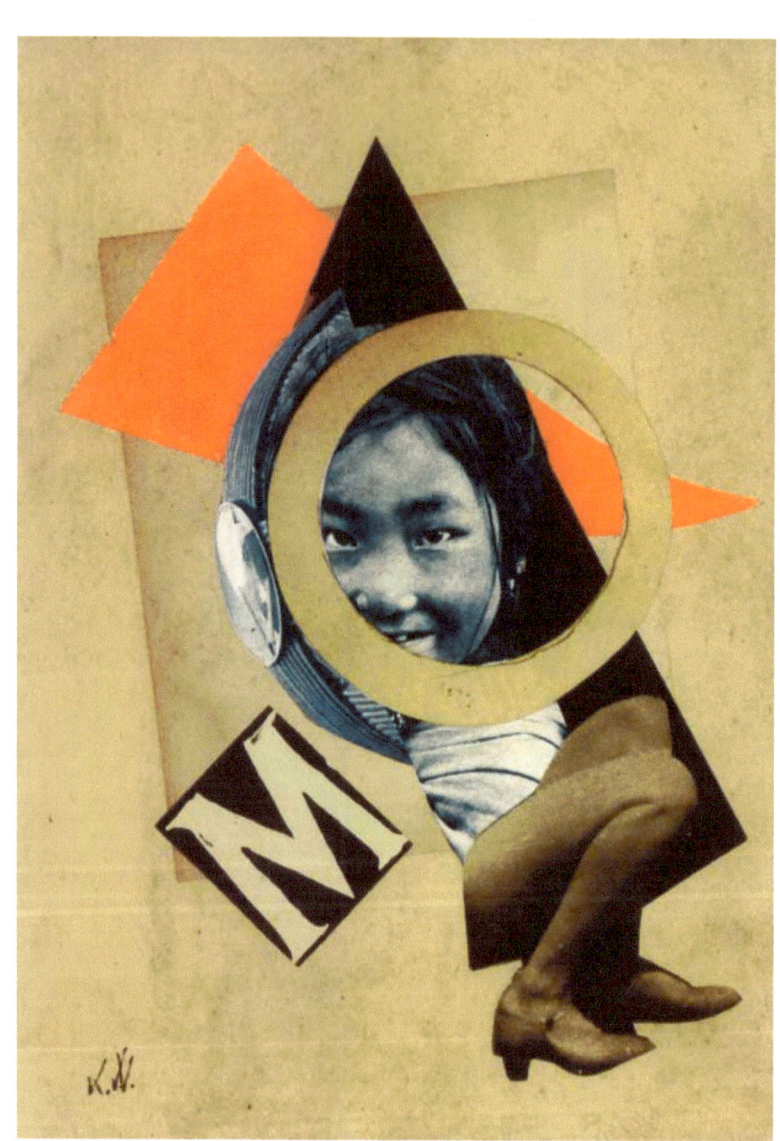

cad as dóibh
ní anoir ná aniar a tháinig siad . . .
gaotha an domhain

they come from nowhere
winds of the earth . . .
neither east nor west

laochra
is banlaochra an domhain—
carn mór geal-chnámh

heroes
and heroines of old—
mountain of shiny bones

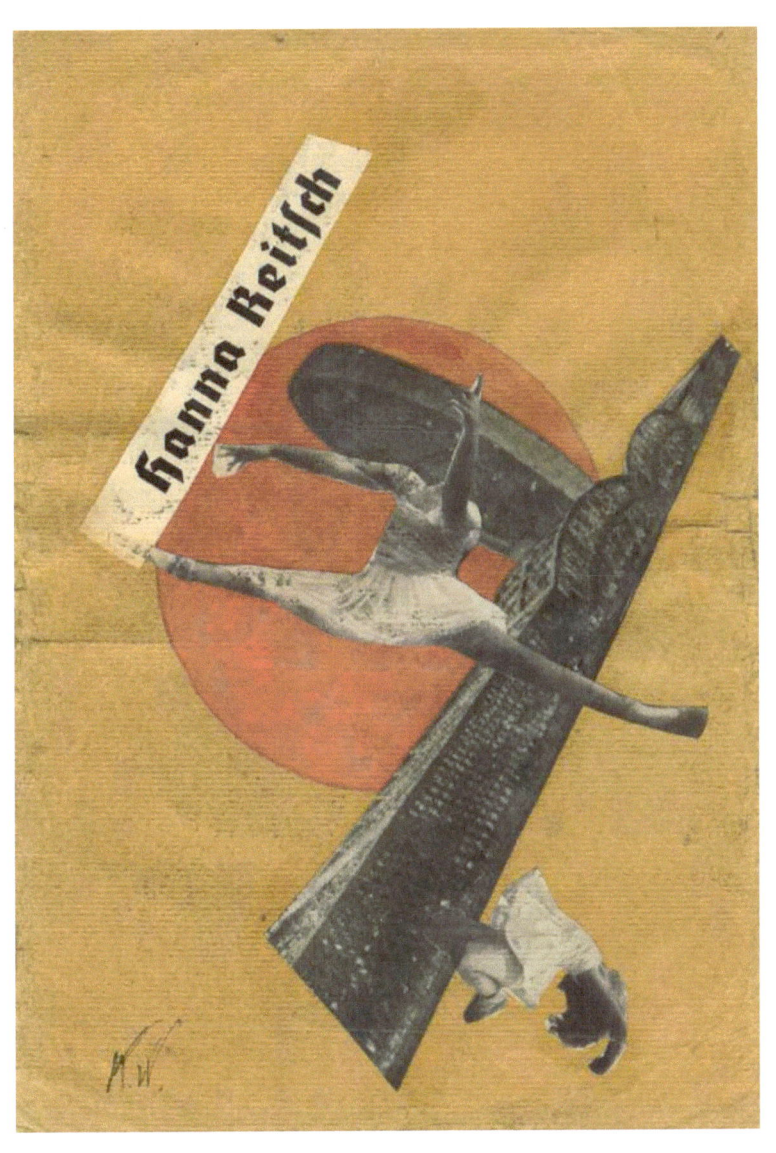

siopa leabhar—
rannóg an haiku á lorg
ag snáthaid an phúca

bookshop
looking for the haiku section—
a daddy-long-legs

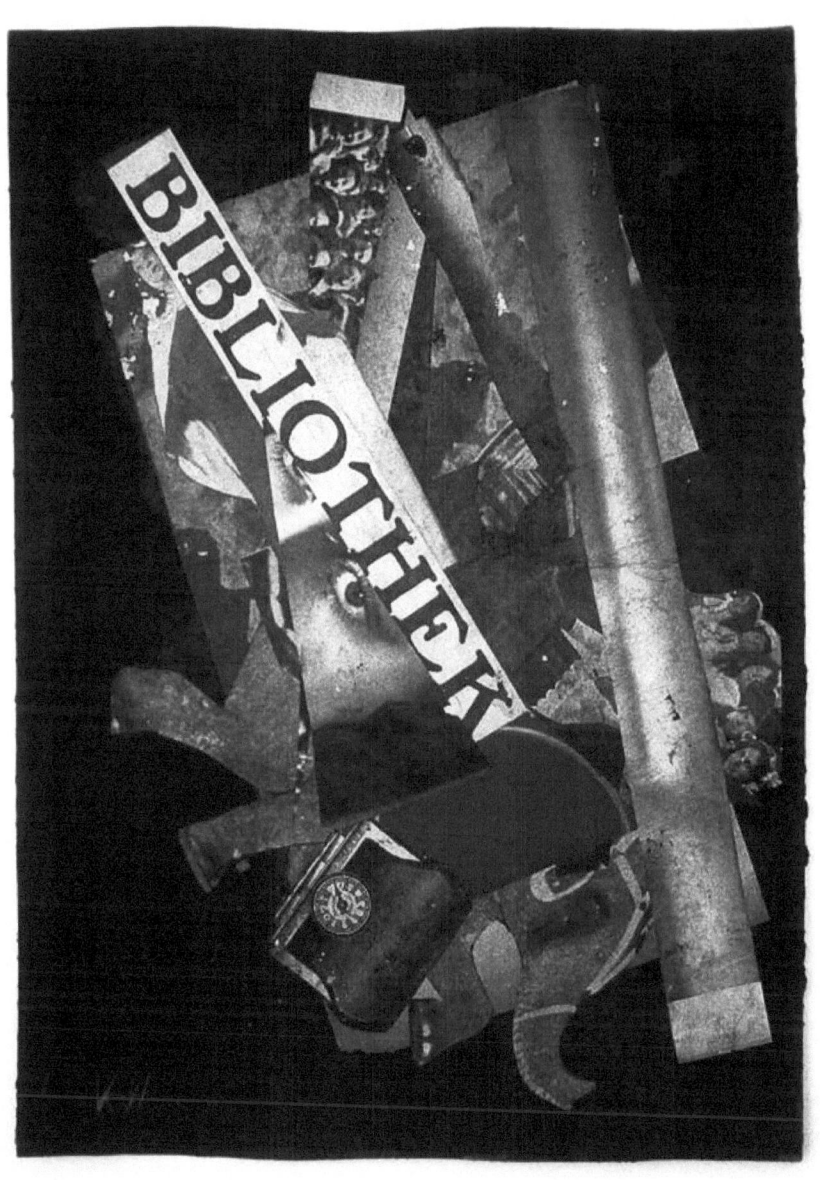

"Out of the fullness of this presence of mind, disturbed by no ulterior motive, the artist who is released from all attachment must practice his art."

Eugen Herrrigel

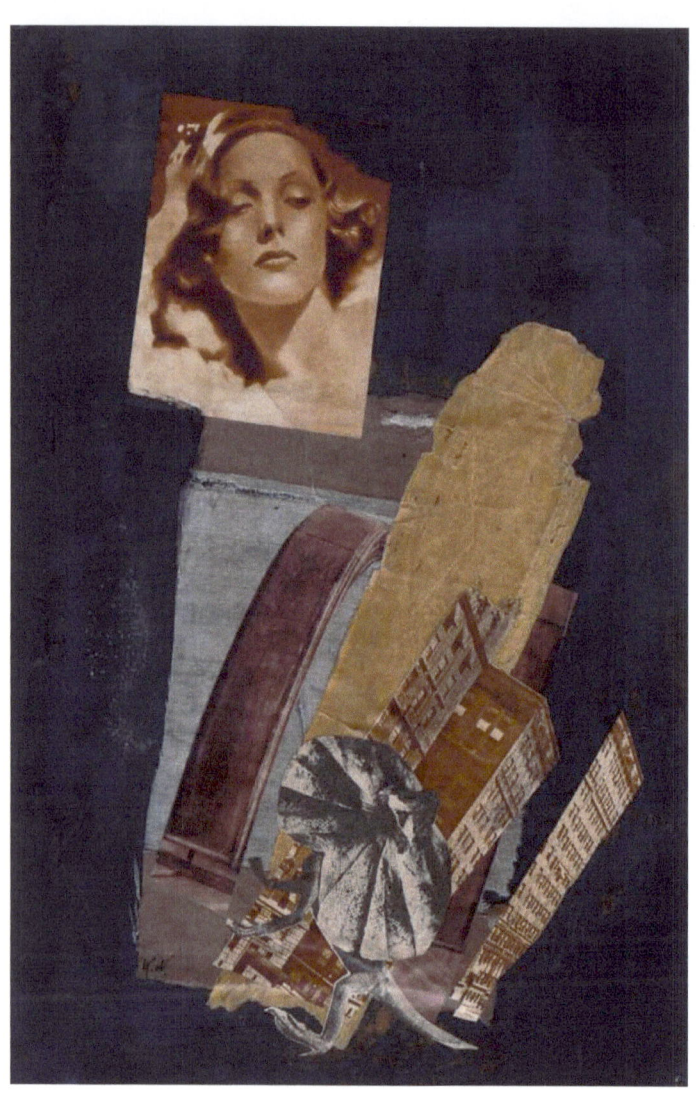

deacair tuiscint 'fháil
ar leabhar gearrthóg ár n-óige . . .
sneachta sa chlós

hard to understand
the scrap-book of our youth . . .
snow in the yard

nathair ina codladh sa zú—
an bhfeicfimid ár ngarchlann
arís

in the zoo a sleeping snake—
will we see our grandchildren
again

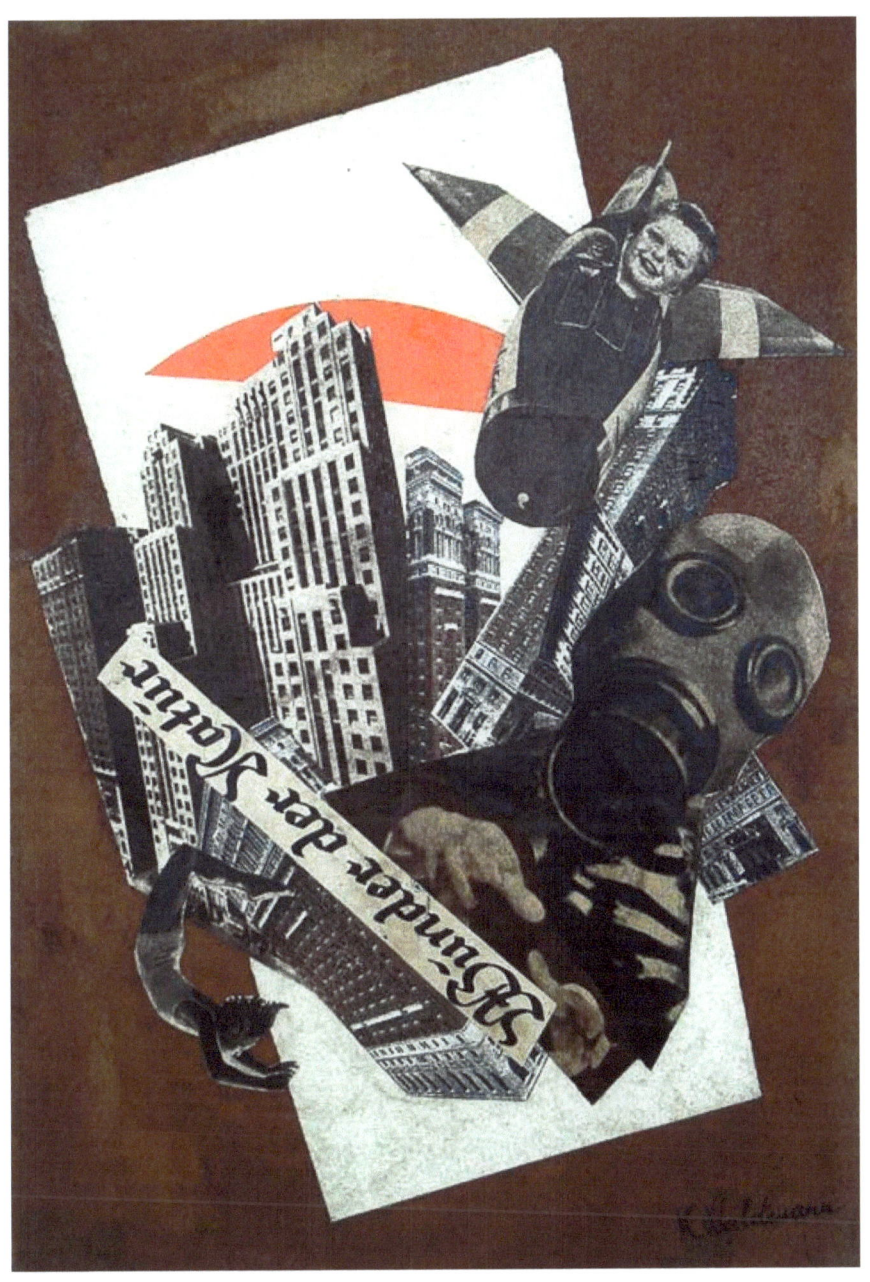

níl ann ach haiku—
ná síl gur chugat féin
é

it's just a haiku—
don't take it
personally

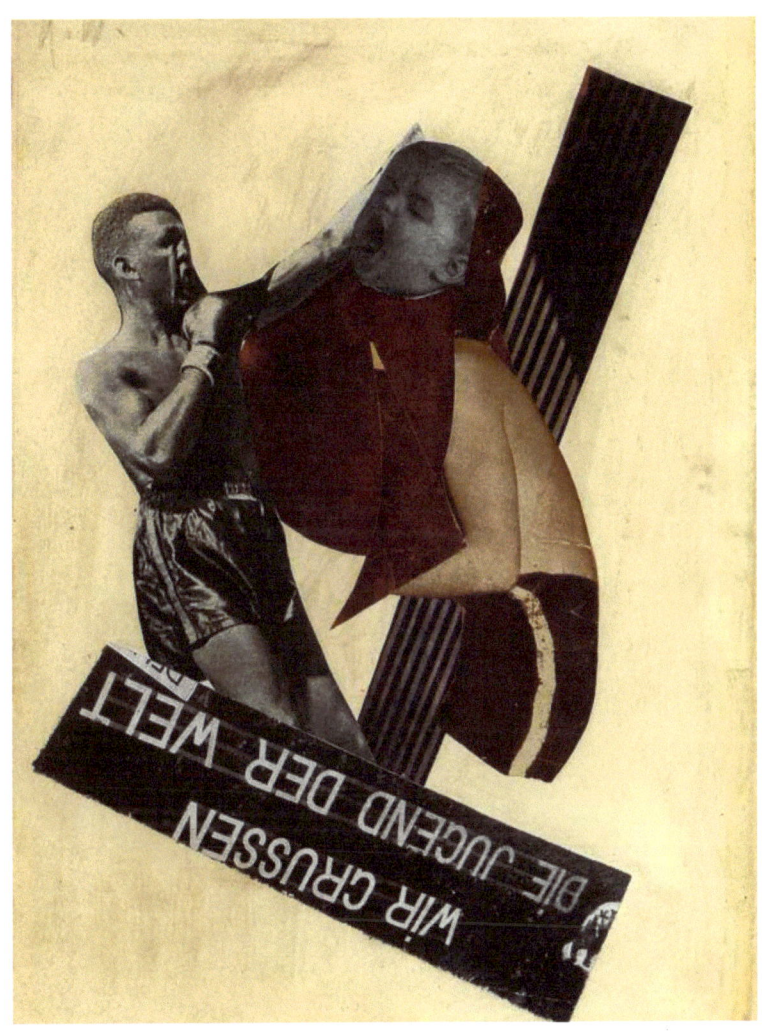

leoithne mhaidine—
géarghá le hoileán
trópaiceach

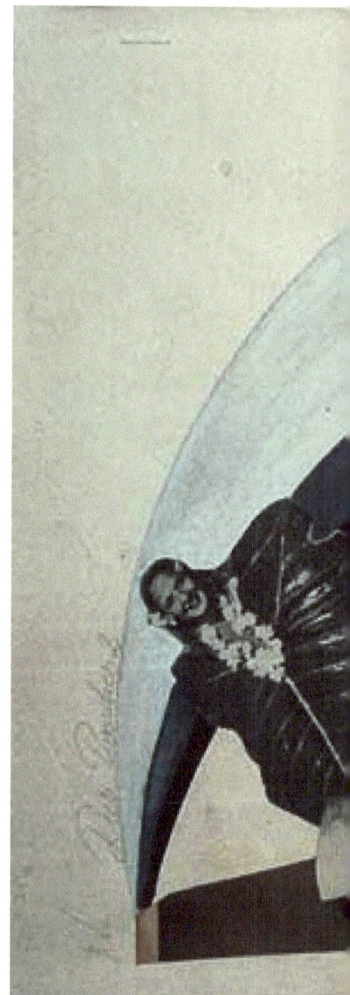

morning breeze—
desperate need for a tropical
island

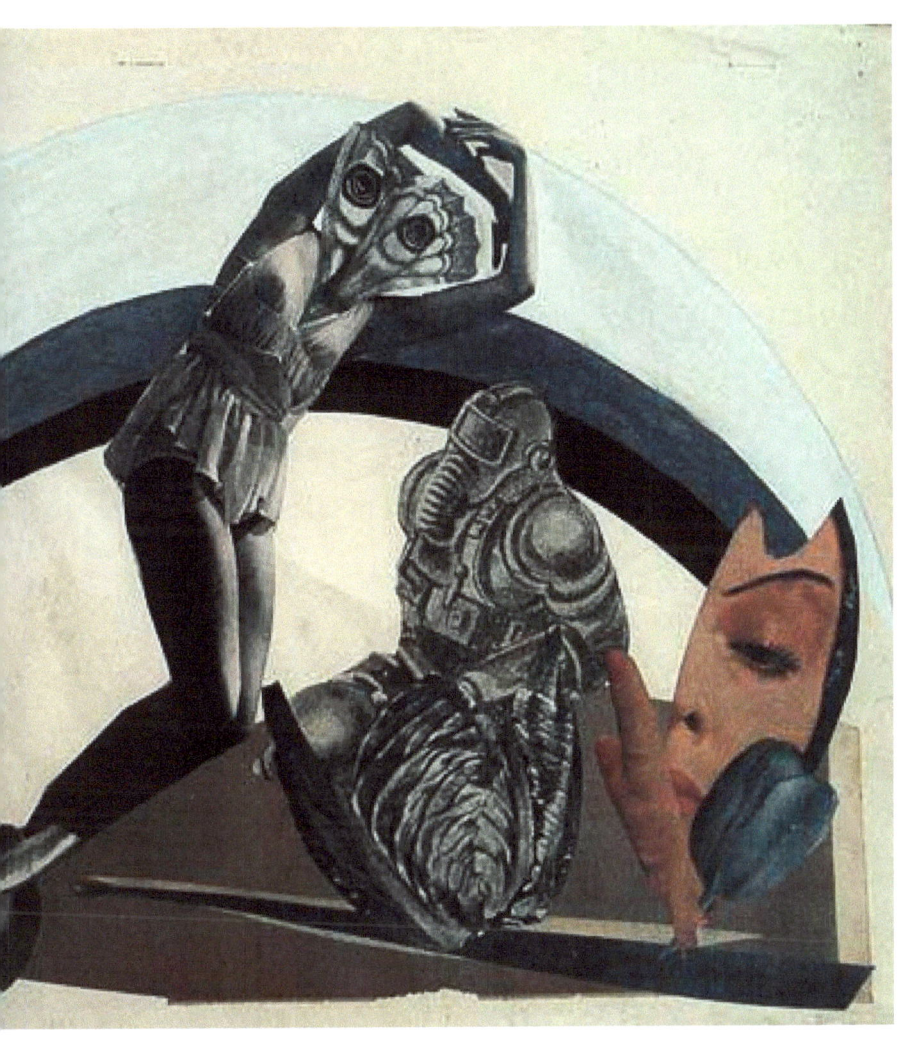

ó
dá mbeadh
tighín agam!

oh
to have
a little house!

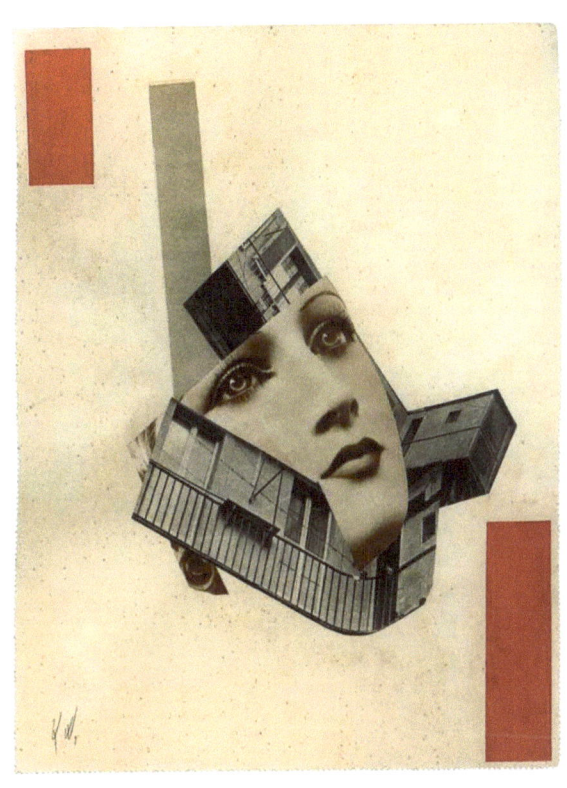

41

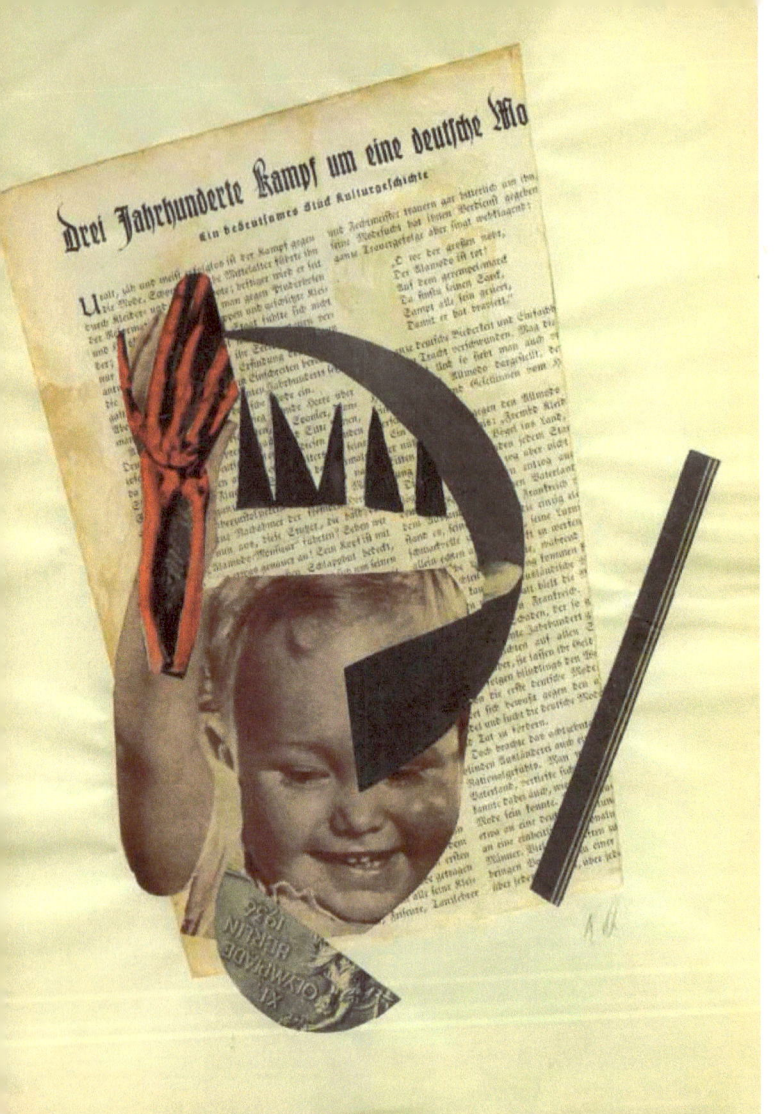

mo leithscéal a dhuine chaoin
cá bhfuil an tír faoi mhil
is faoi bhainne

excuse me kind sir
where is the land of milk
and honey

maidin fhómhair . . .
an uile ní
á scaoileadh

autumn morning . . .
the unravelling of all
things

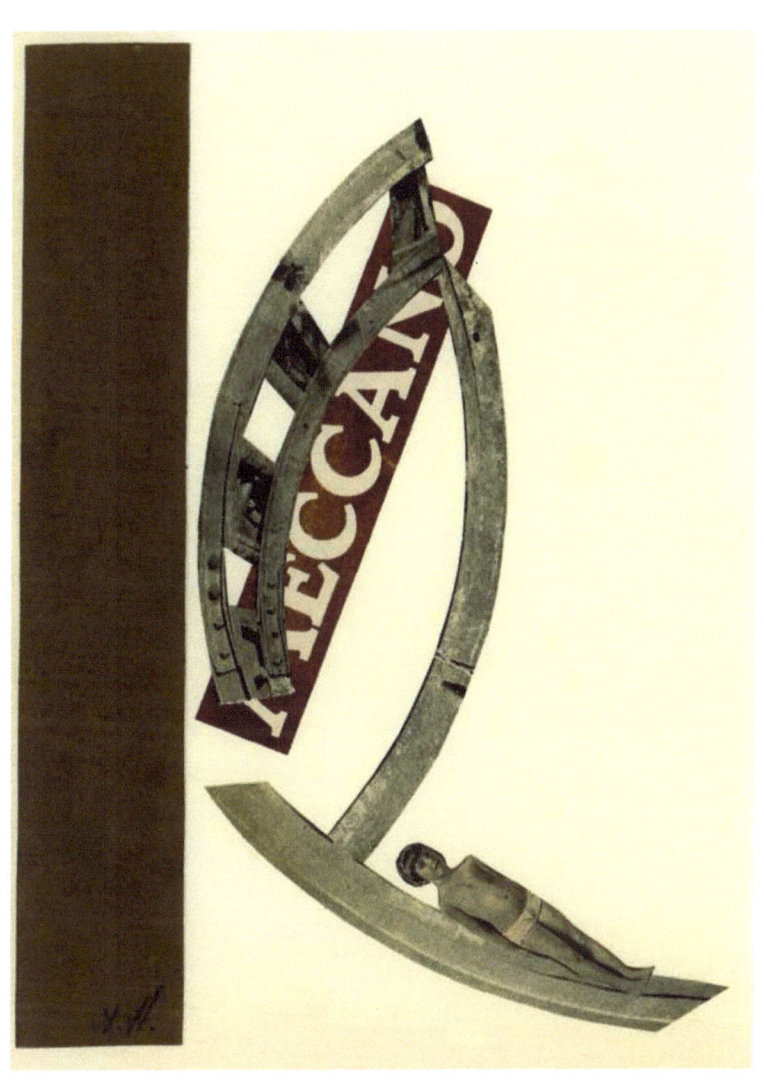

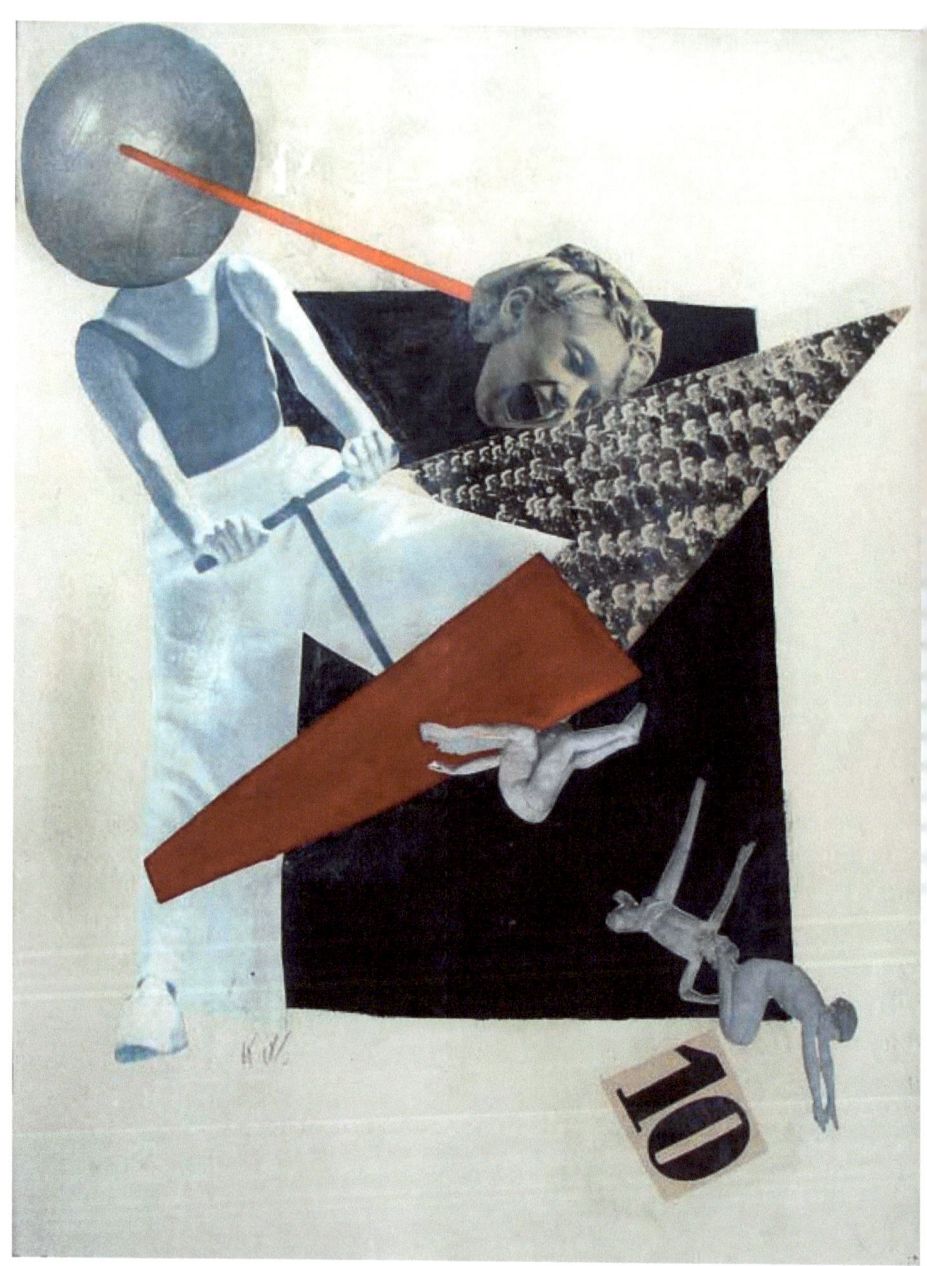

an stair . . .
ag tarlú gan fhios dúinn
is sinn tumtha inti

history . . .
not knowing it's happening
we plunge into it

seangán ar phár
chomh bog bídeach—
mharófaí dá n-aistreofaí é

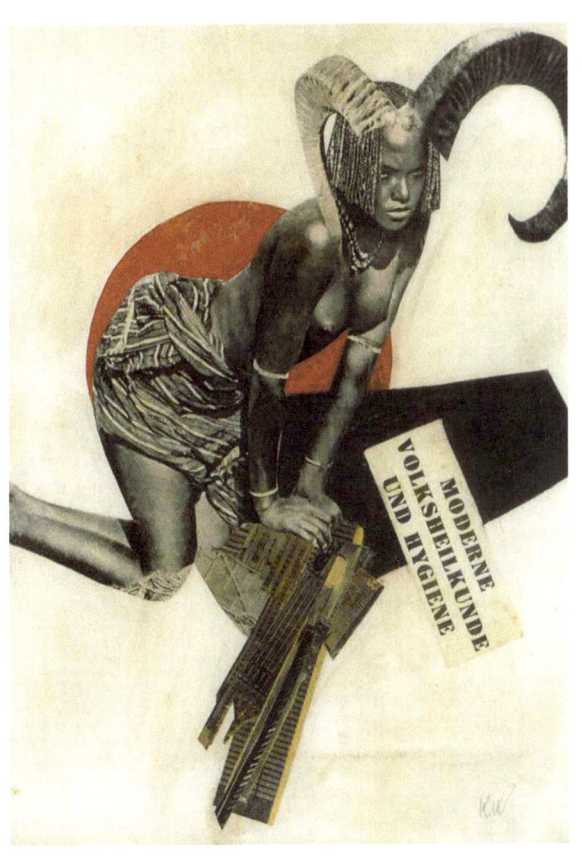

insect on a page
so soft and small—
to move it would be its death

trapaigh ag dul i léig
ní bheidh aon dea-bheoir ann—
fual ar fad

trappists are dying out
there'll be no more beer left—
all piss

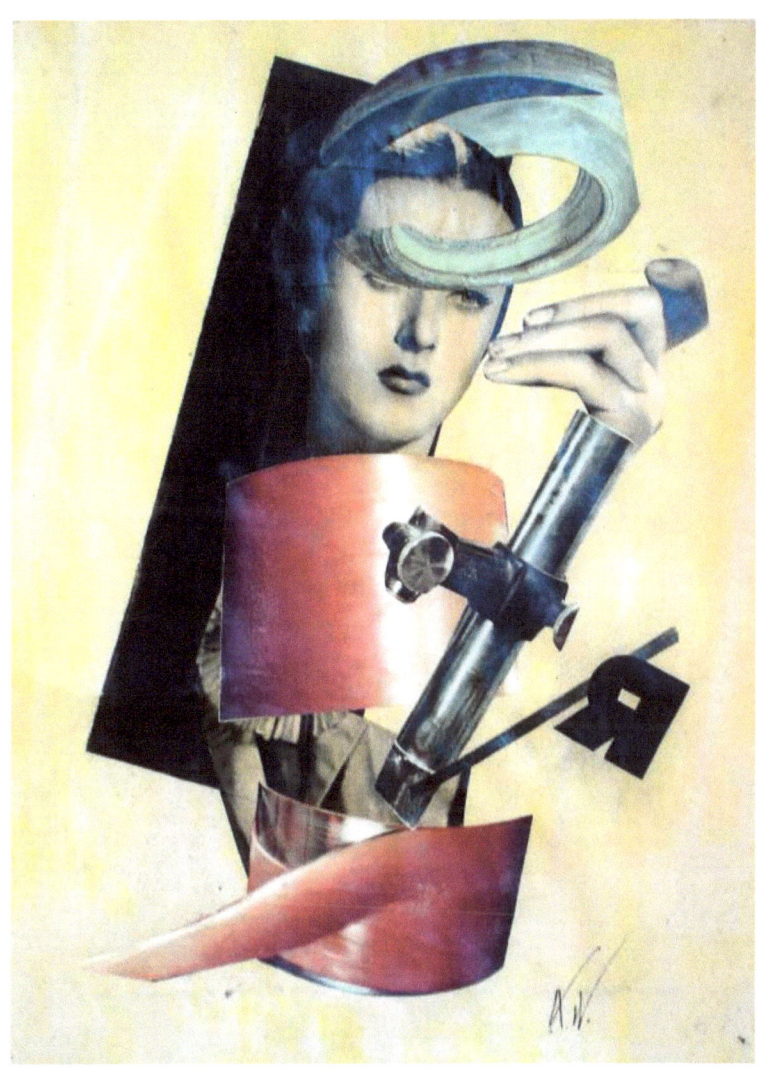

"He grows daily more capable of following any inspiration without technical effort, and also of letting inspiration come to him through meticulous observation."

Eugen Herrigel

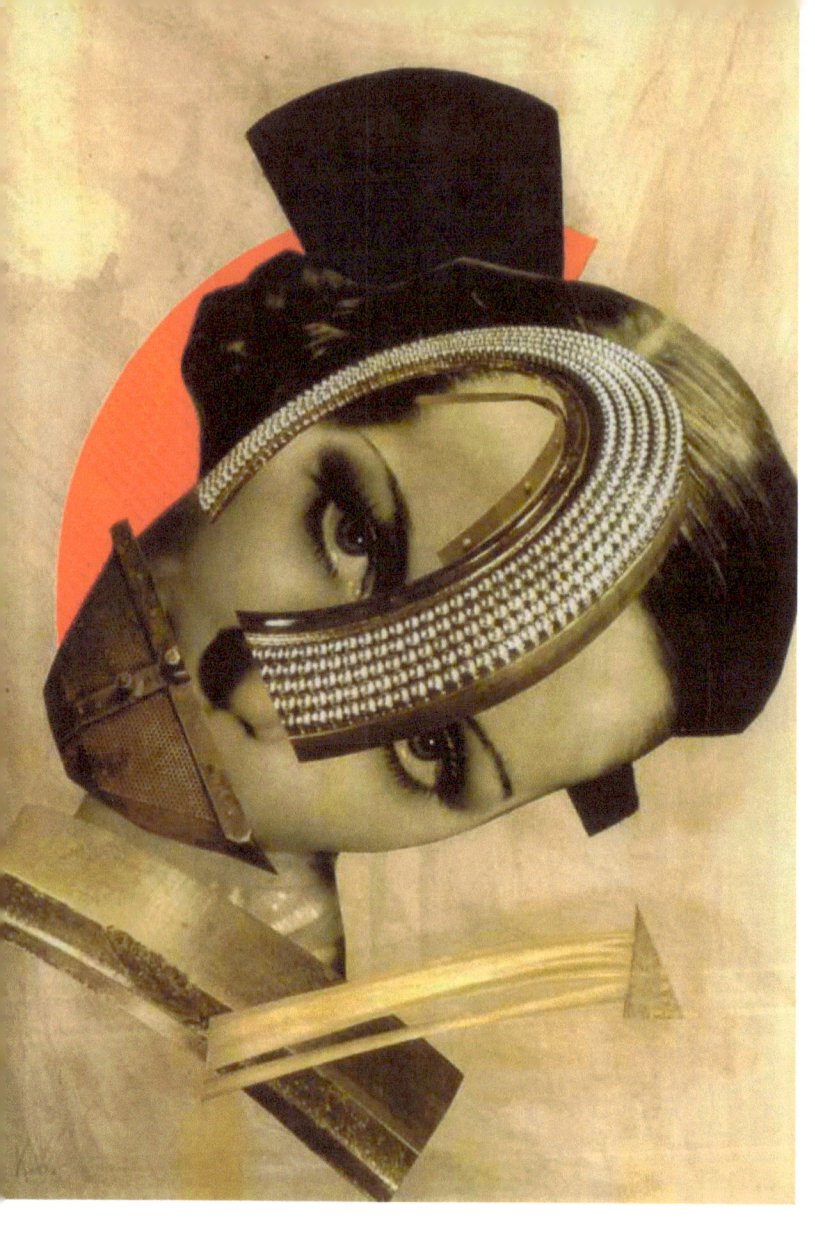

smearadh
san áit a raibh seangán—
dorchaíonn an intinn

a smudge
where an insect was—
darkening the mind

bheith id' shioráf
is rith glan amach as do . . .
as do chraiceann

to be a giraffe
and run straight out of one's . . .
out of one's skin

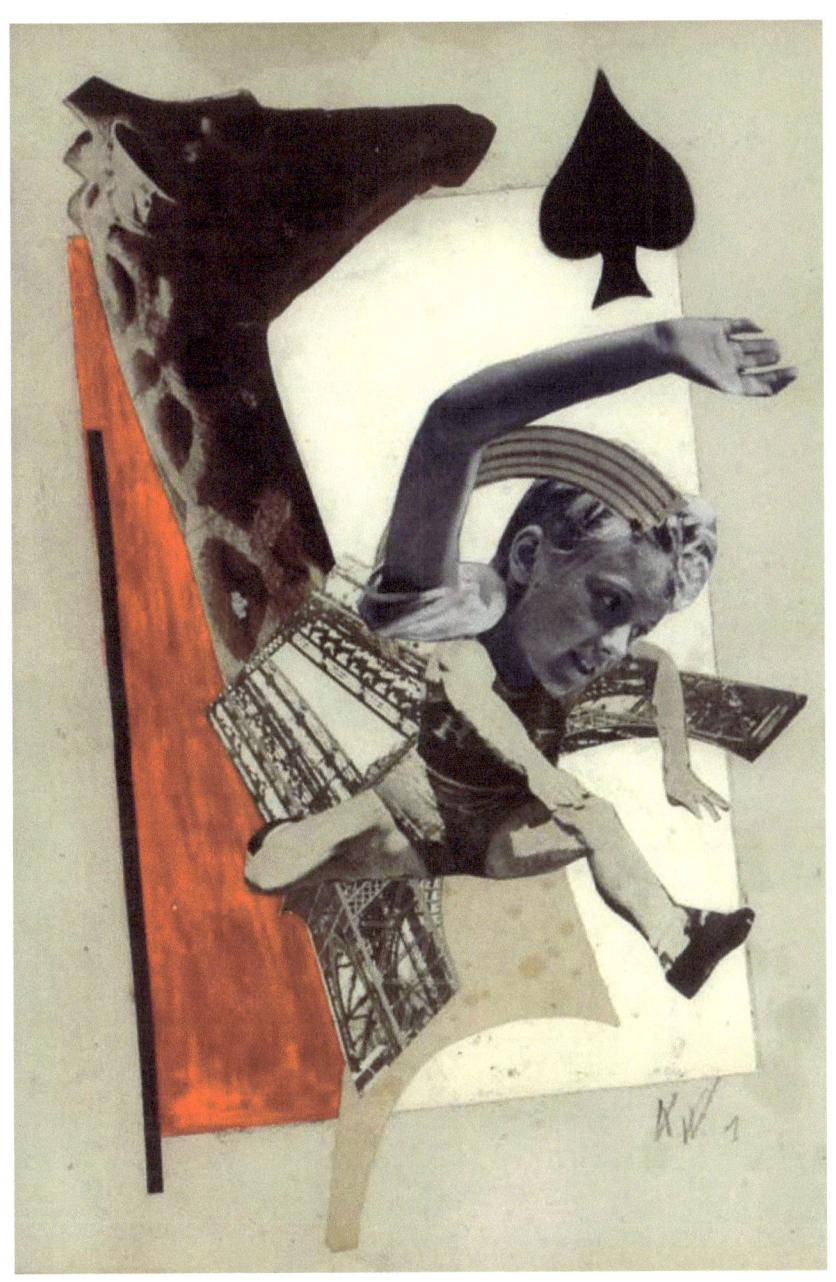

48

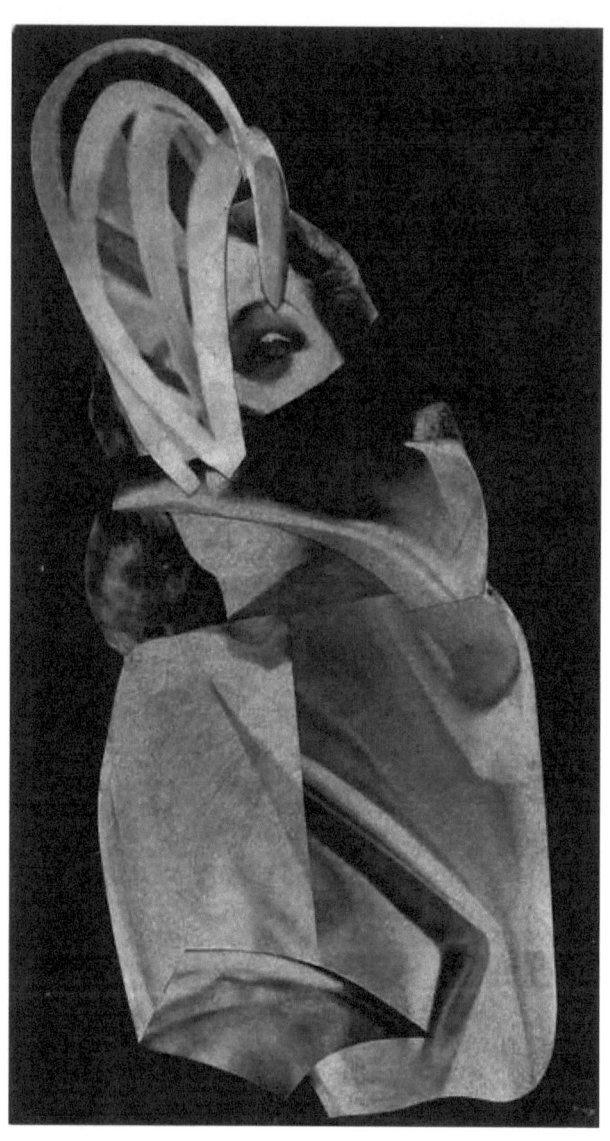

maidin ghlas . . .
ar dhiallait na rothar go léir
drúcht

grey morning . . .
on all of the bicycle saddles
dew

cá bhfuil an tsaoirse
cad is saoirse ann
braon báistí

where is liberty
what is it
a raindrop

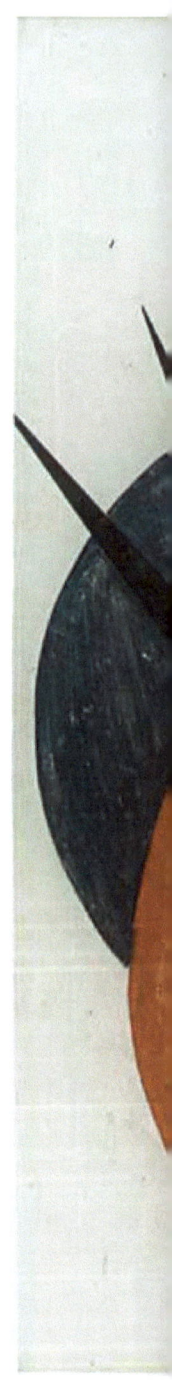

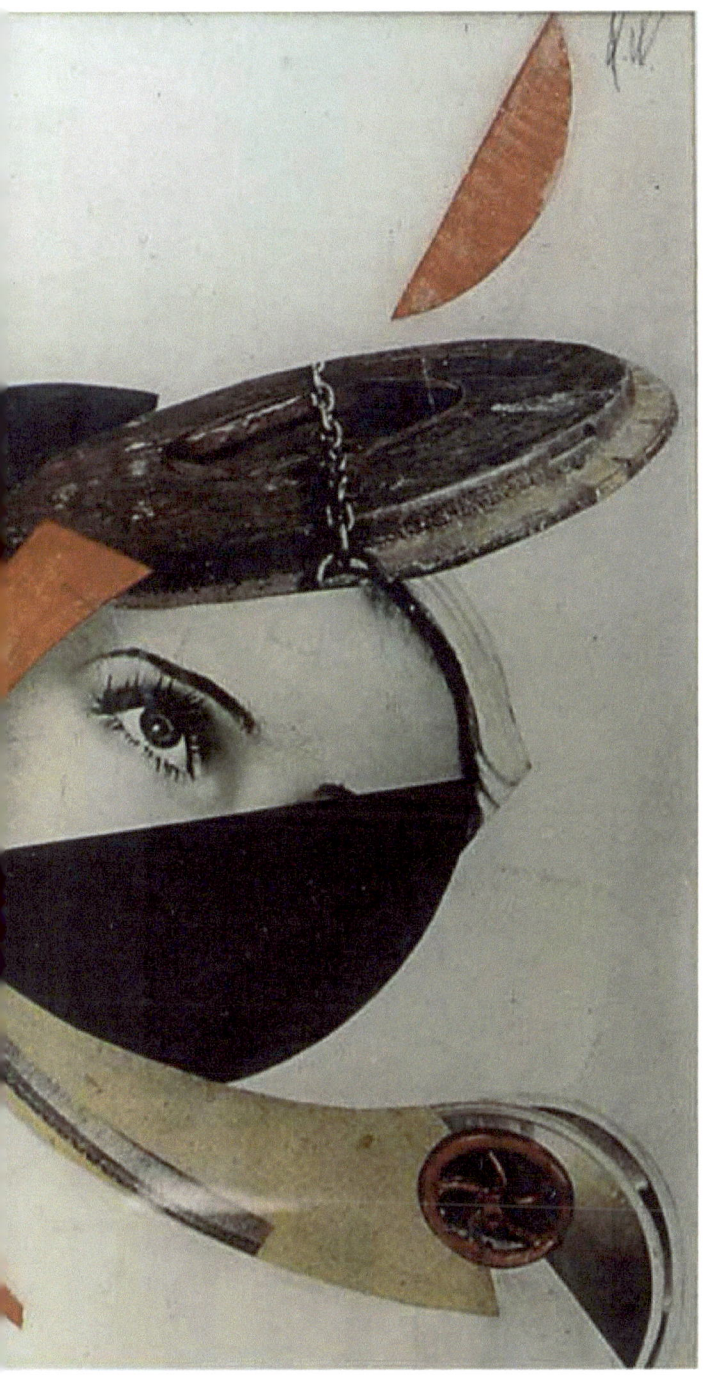

labhair liom
le do dhá shúil amháin . . .
deireadh an tsamhraidh

speak to me only
with thine eyes . . .
end of summer

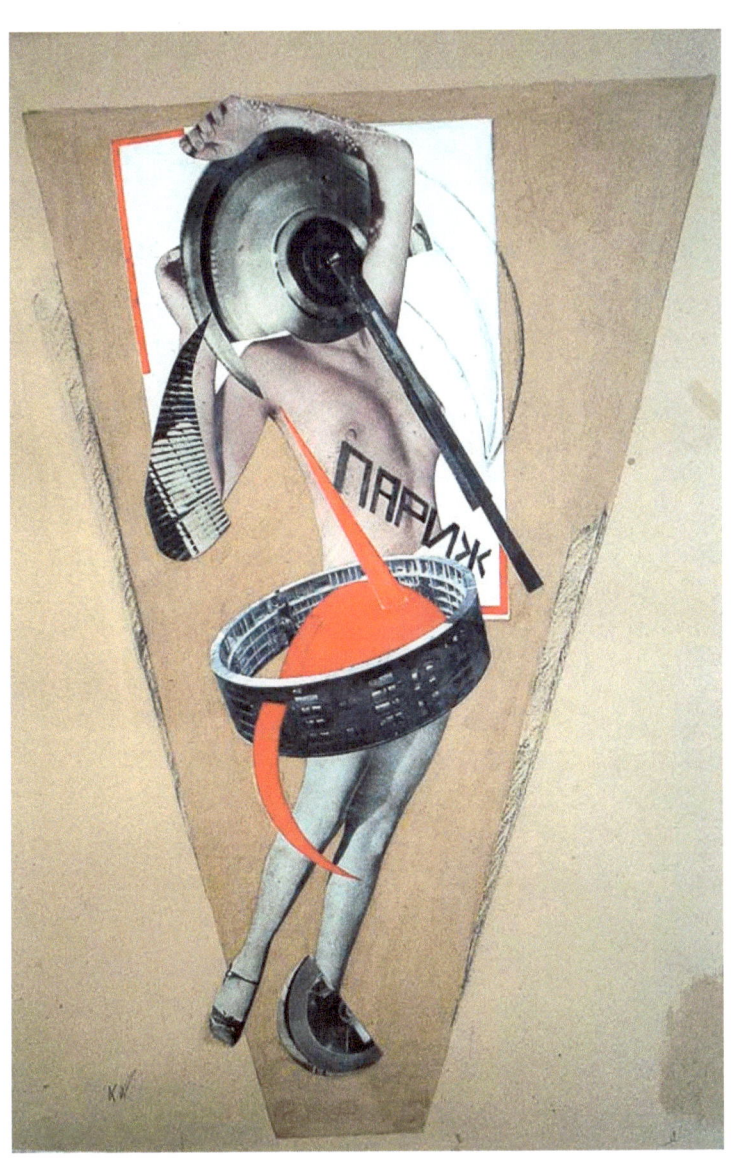

maidin gheimhridh—
amhrán na farraige
garbh fuar

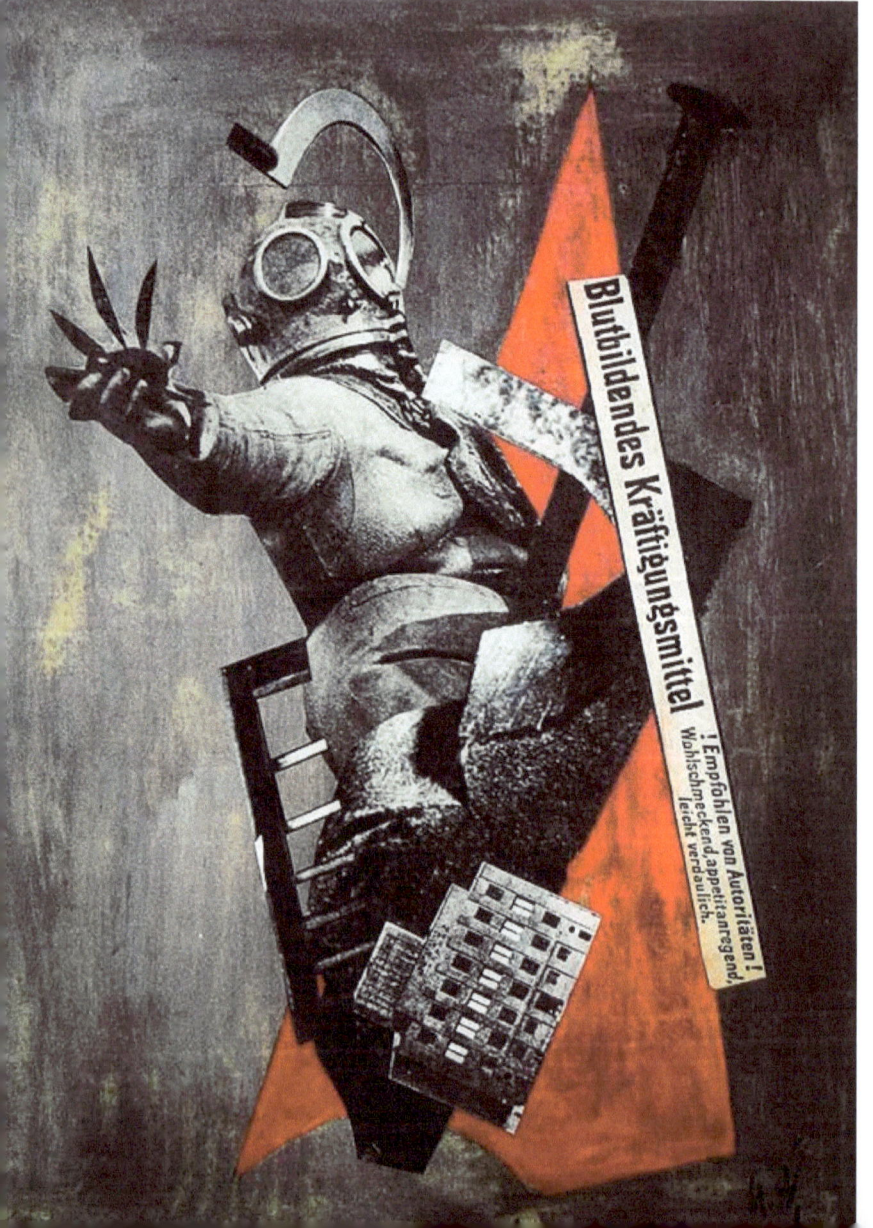

wintry morning—
song of the sea
harsh and cold

an tíogar ionam—
ní fhaca sé fós
an tíogar ionatsa

the tiger in me—
it has yet to see
the tiger in you

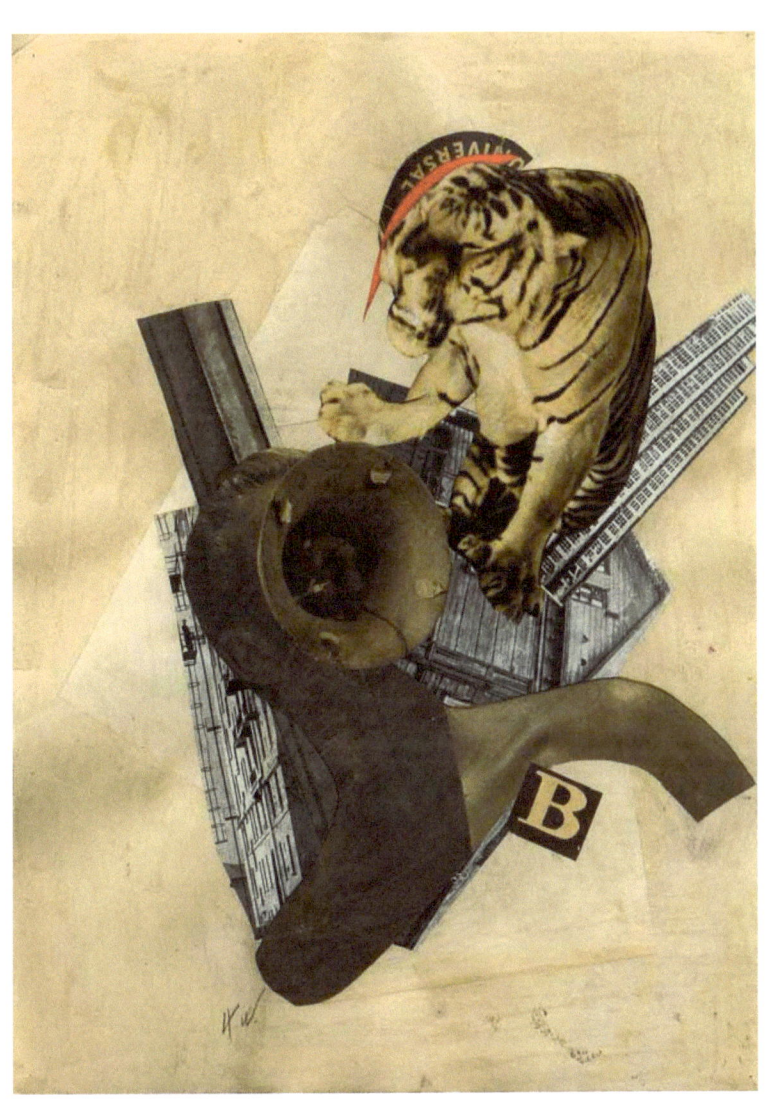

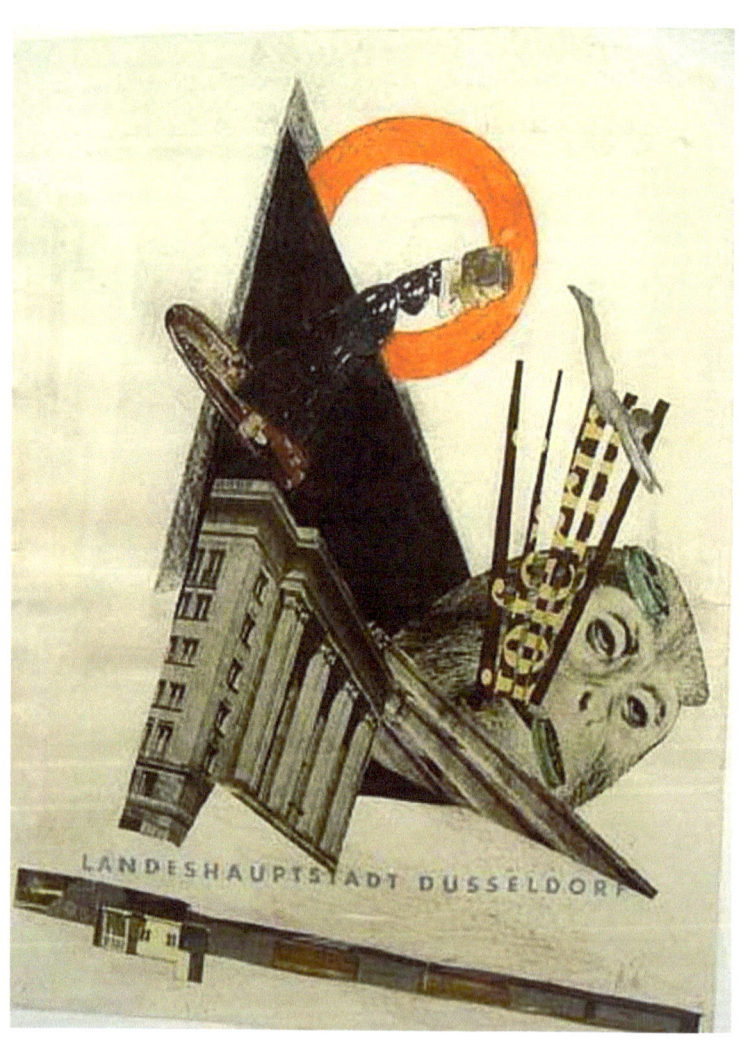

lucht an domhain seo—
greim gruama
ar an gcruinne ghuagach acu

terrestrials . . .
grimly holding on
to this floating world

her bare shoulders
that once glistened
with my tears

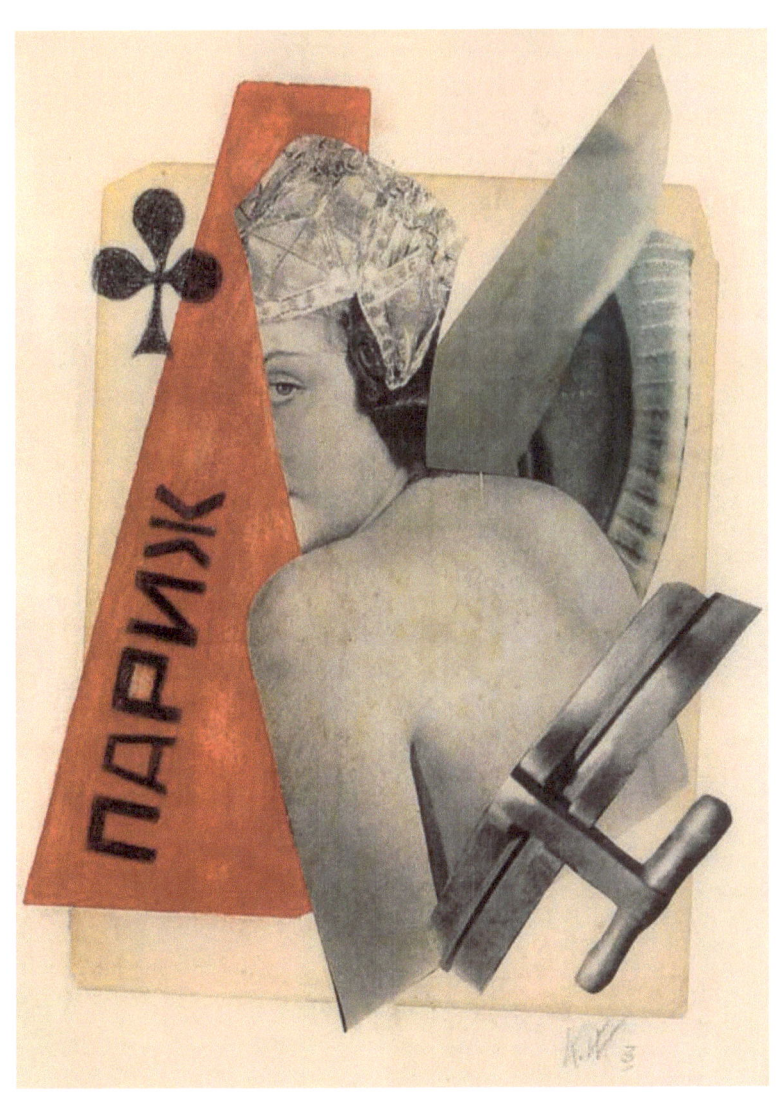

a guaillí loma
is iad ag glioscarnach tráth
lem' dheora

suirí . . .
mar do leath
do pholláirí

lovemaking . . .
the way your nostrils
flared

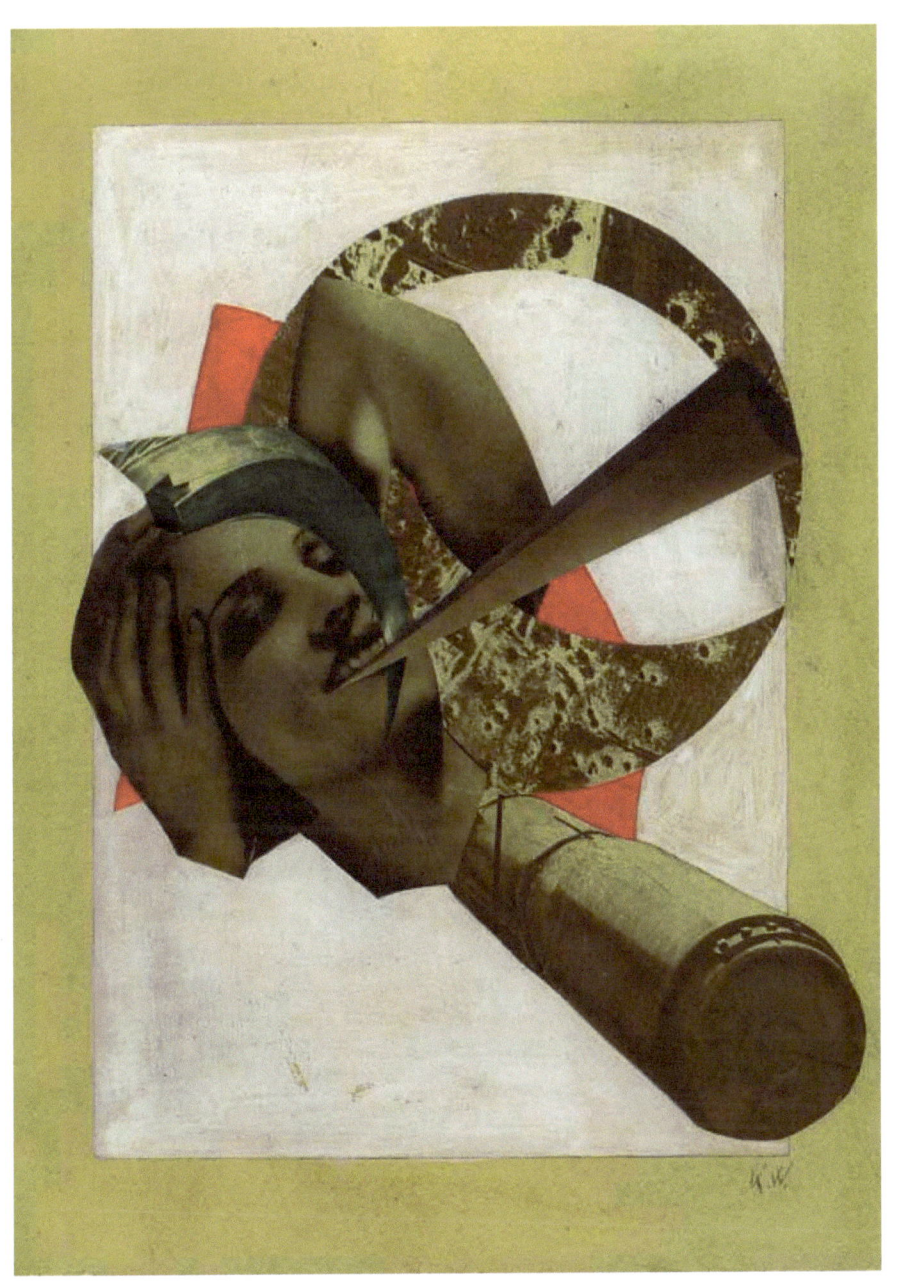

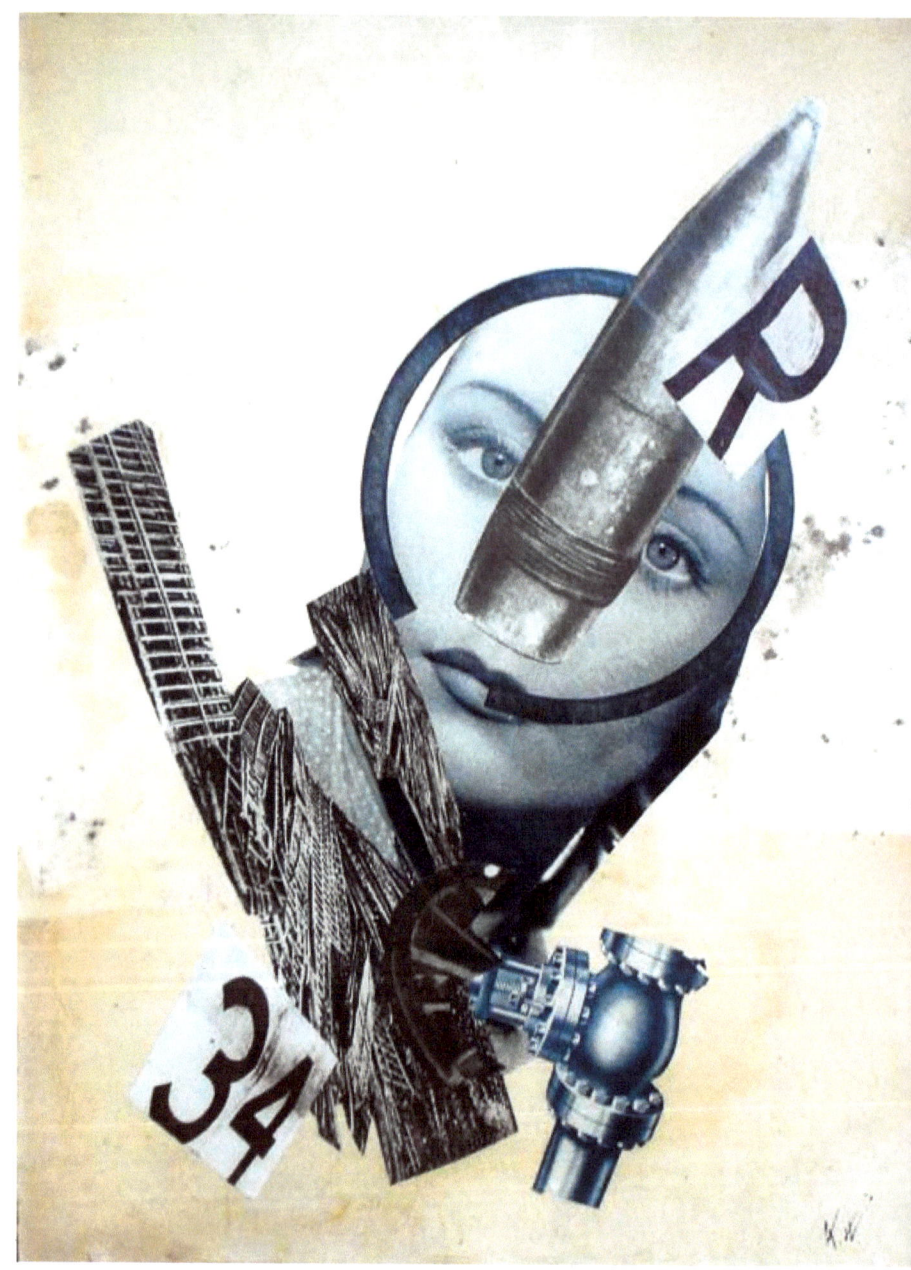

geimhreadh . . .
aistear traenach
níor fhill tú riamh

winter . . .
you took a train
and never returned

"Don't think of what you have to do, don't consider how to carry it out! he exclaimed. The shot will only go smoothly when it takes the archer himself by surprise."

Eugen Herrigel

á gcur le chéile arís—
codanna éagsúla
díom féin

putting them together again—
bits and pieces
of myself

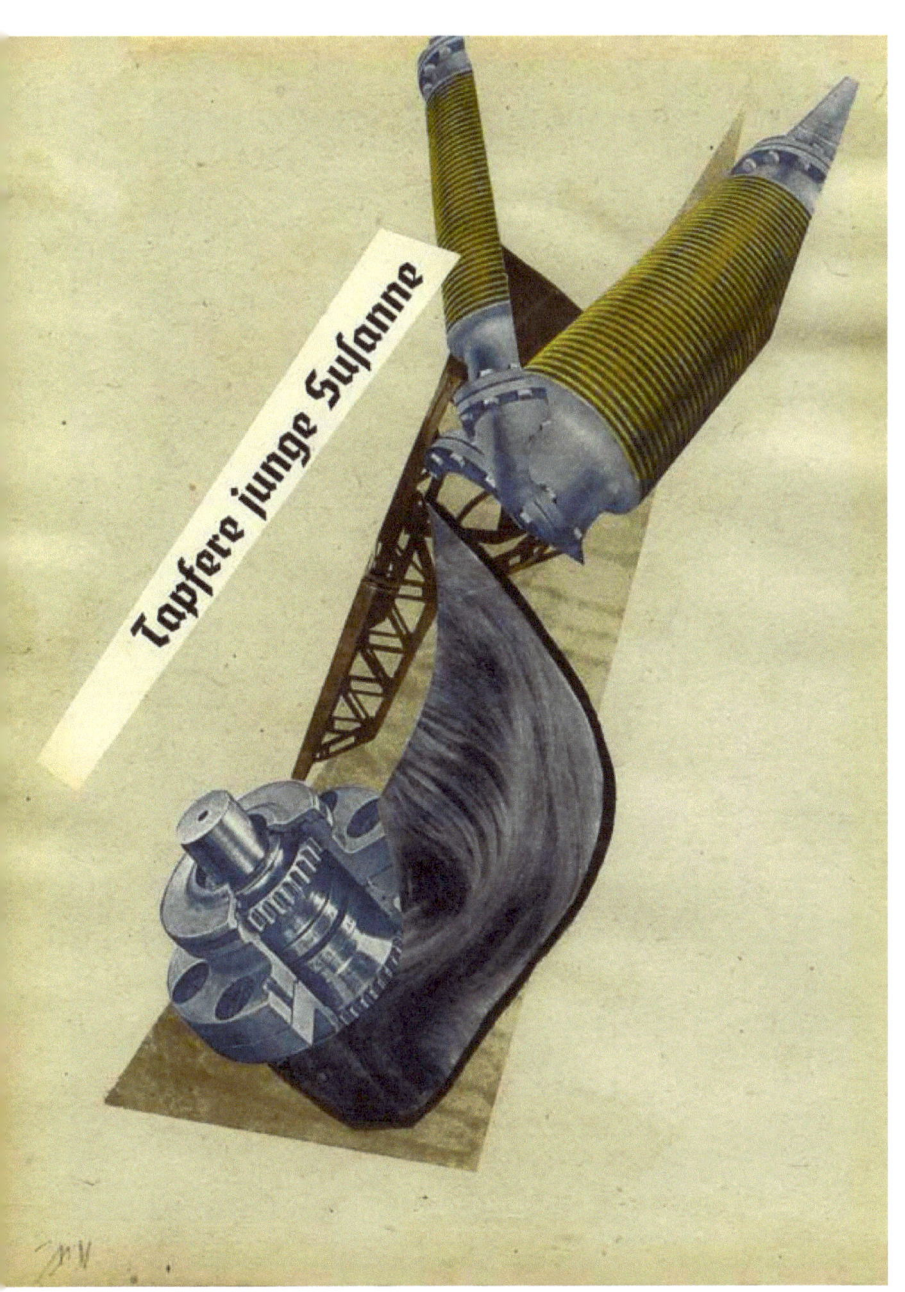

Tapfere junge Susanne

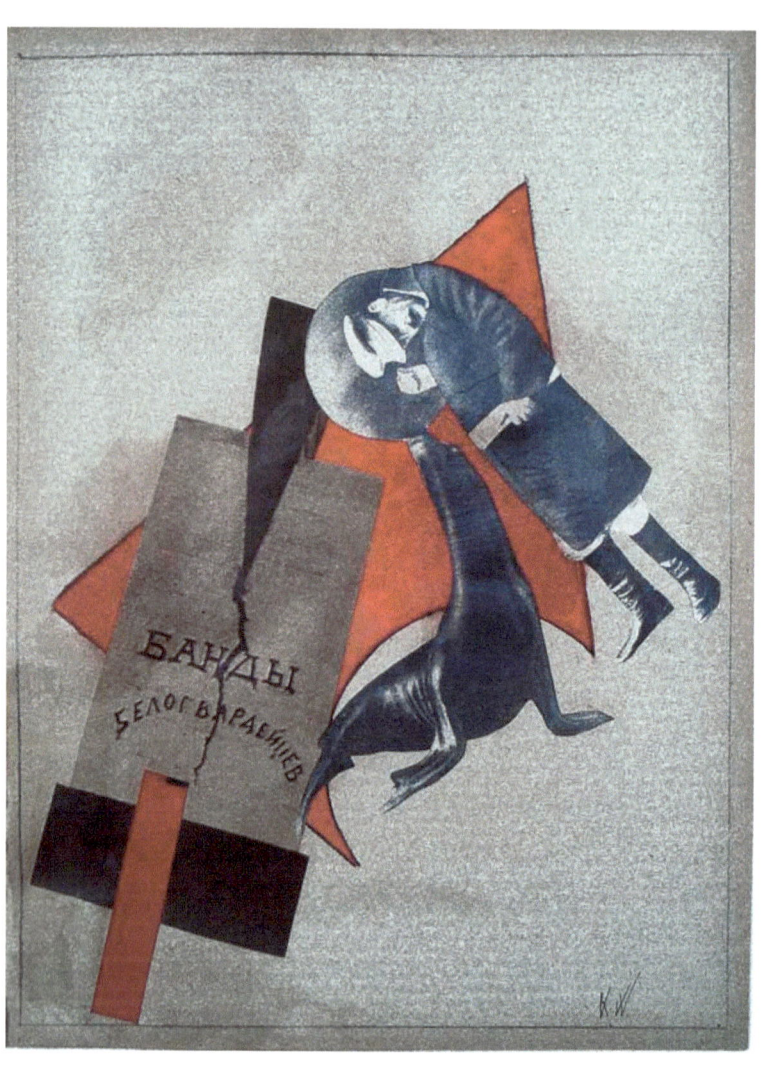

cad ab ea sinn
dá chéile—
rónta otairídeacha

what was i to you
or you to me—
an eared seal

bailc fhuar—
cén mearbhall atá orm
ní mharódh ní ar bith ár ngrá

cold downpour—
who am i kidding
nothing could kill our love

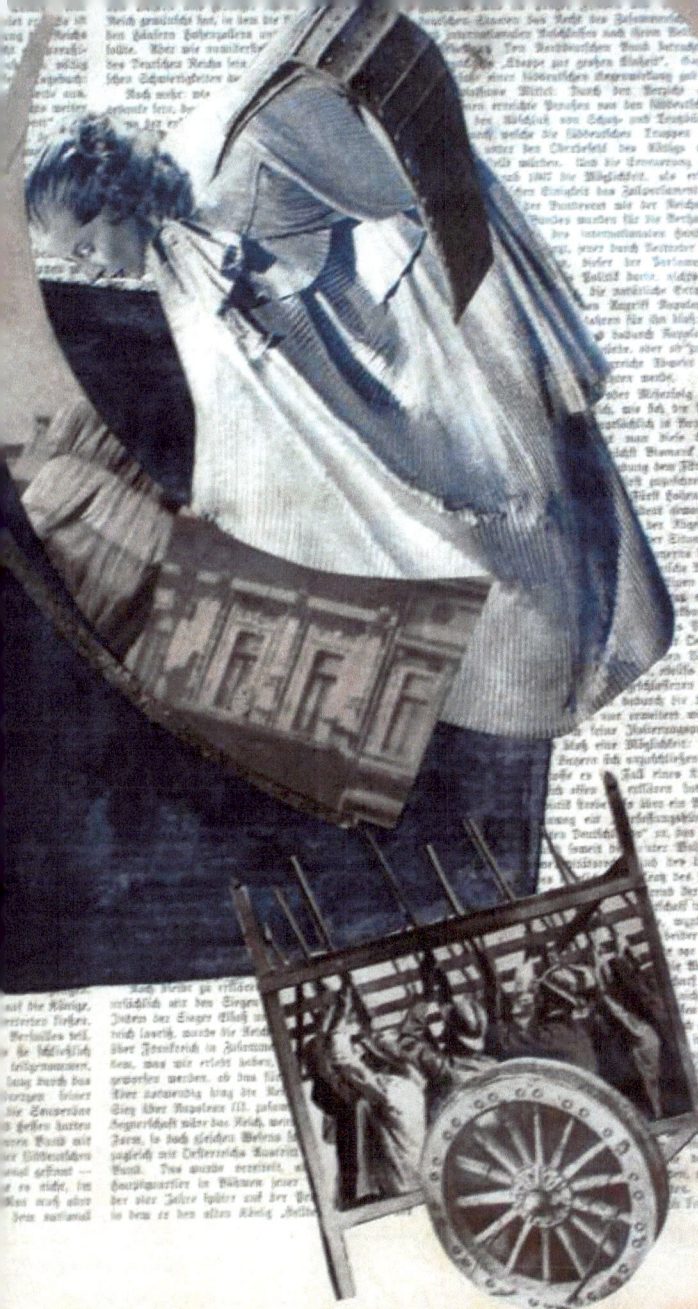

tagann an ghrian amach
leanann an saol—
más féidir saol a thabhairt air

the sun comes out
life goes on—
if you can call it that

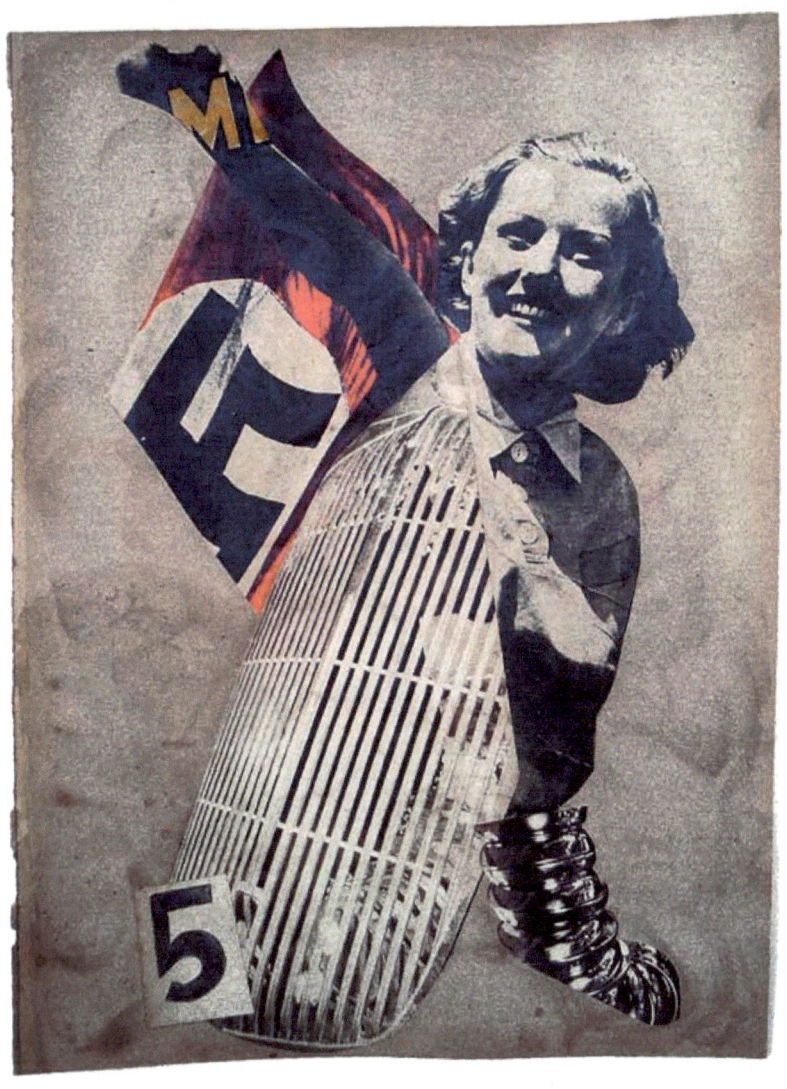

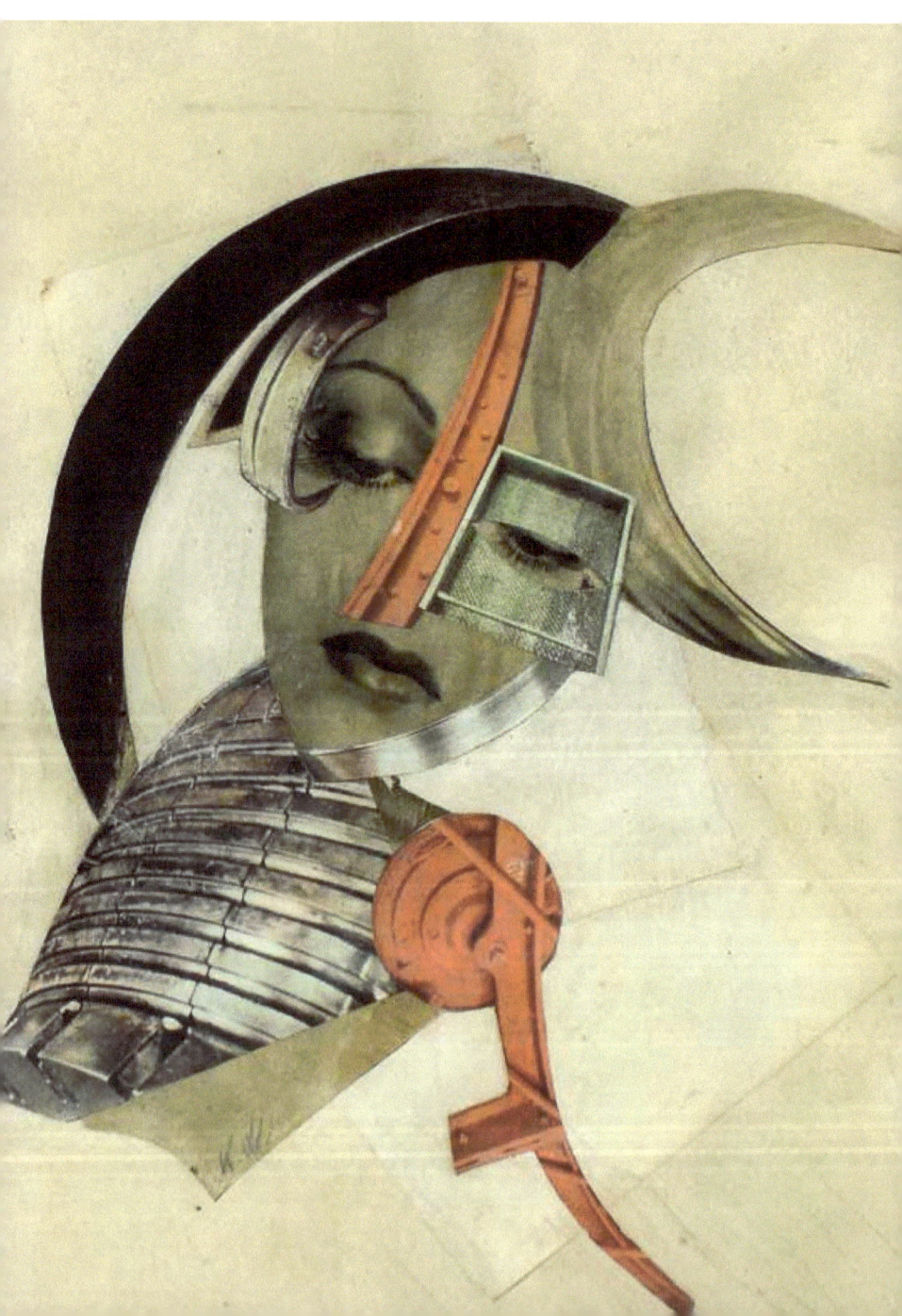

scamaill
ar a n-aistear tuirsiúil . . .
sin mar a bhíonn

clouds
on their weary way . . .
so it goes

labhrann an snag breac
lig dó labhairt in ainm chroim—
ní gá géilleadh dó

the magpie speaks
let him speak for pity's sake—
we need not believe him

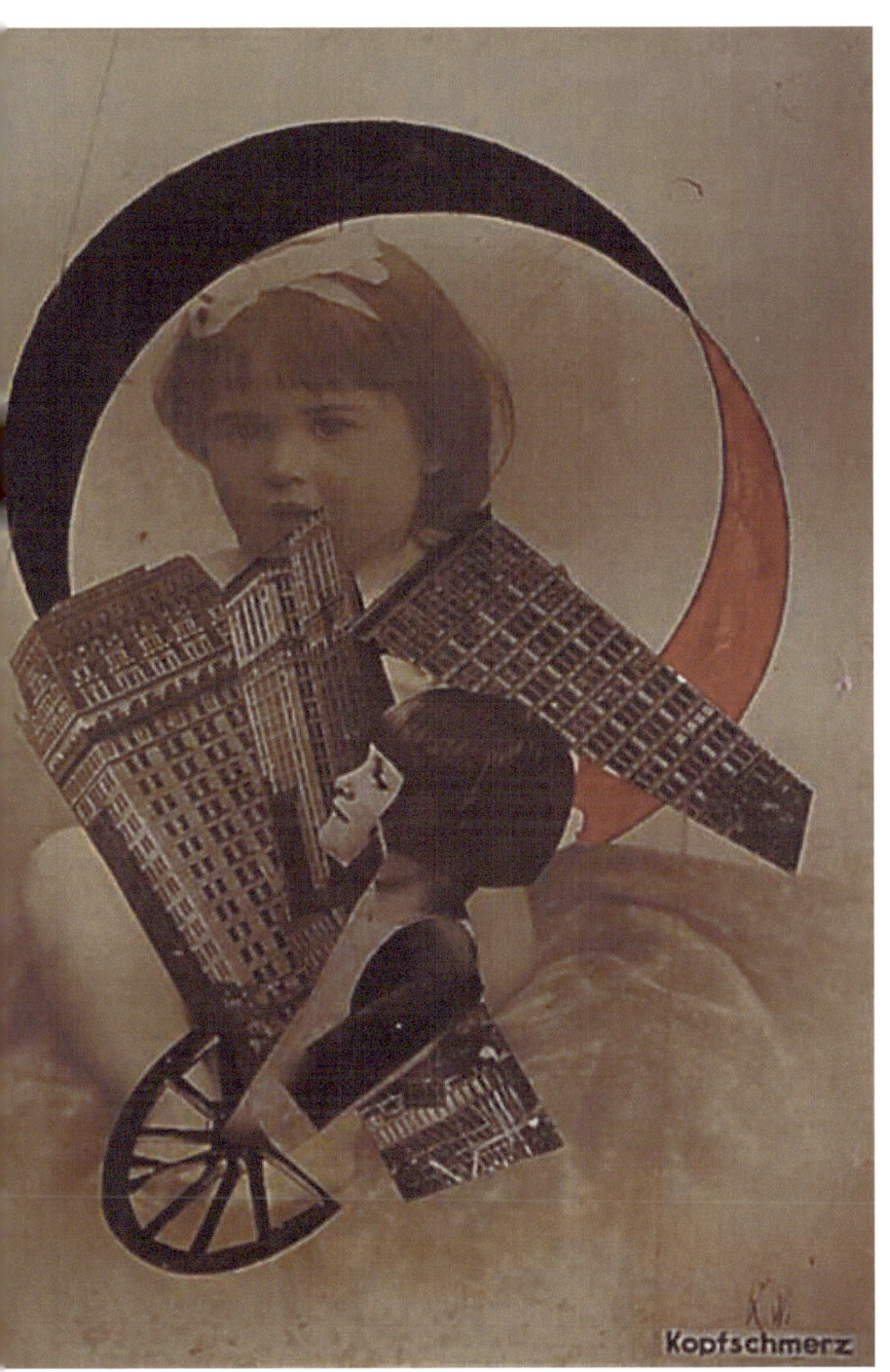

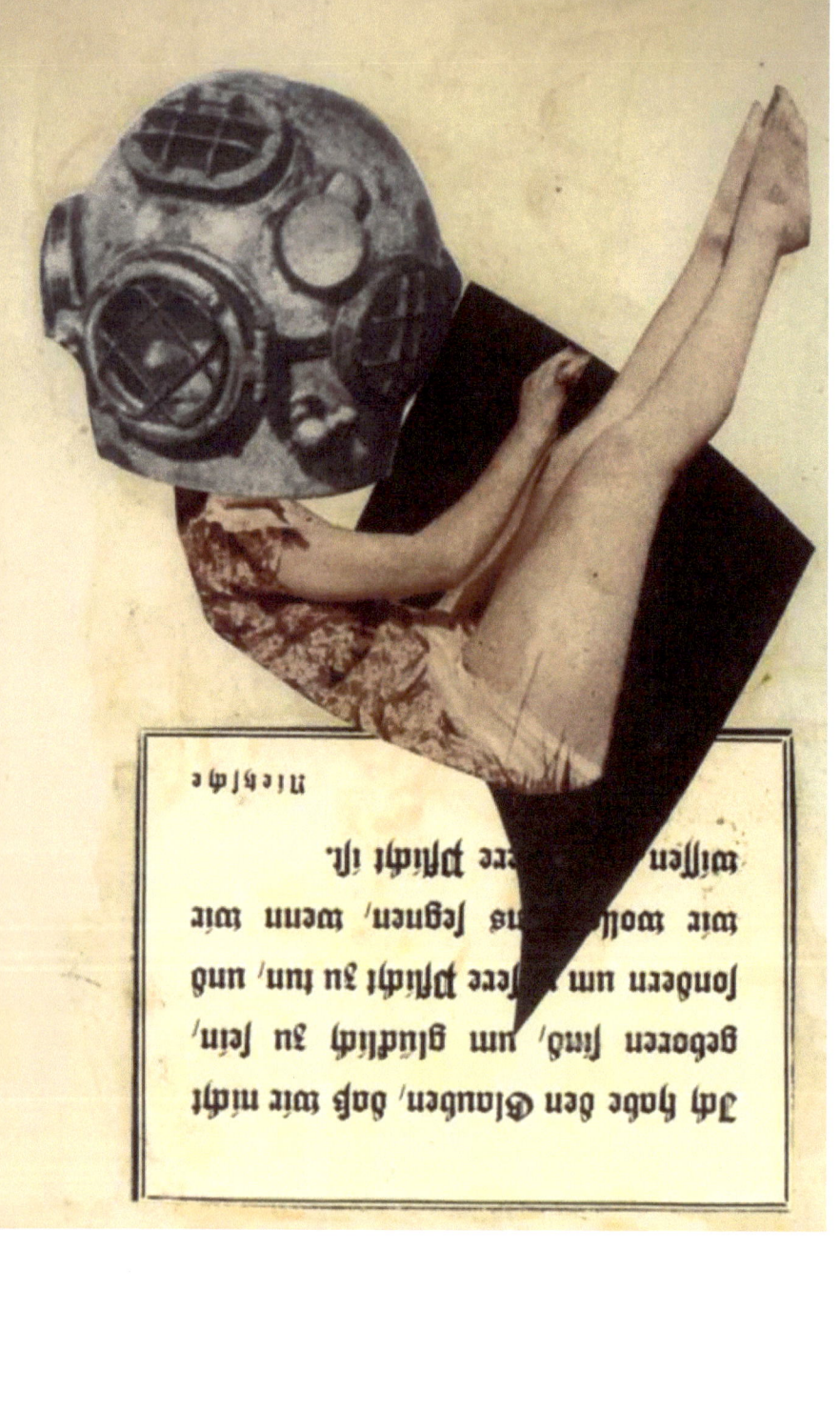

plunging
to find the Self—
who would even think of doing that

tumadh
chun teacht ar an bhFéin—
cé smaoineodh ar a leithéid

coinnímis glan é
níl schweinerei uainn—
an bhfuil

let's keep it clean—
we don't want a schweinerei
do we

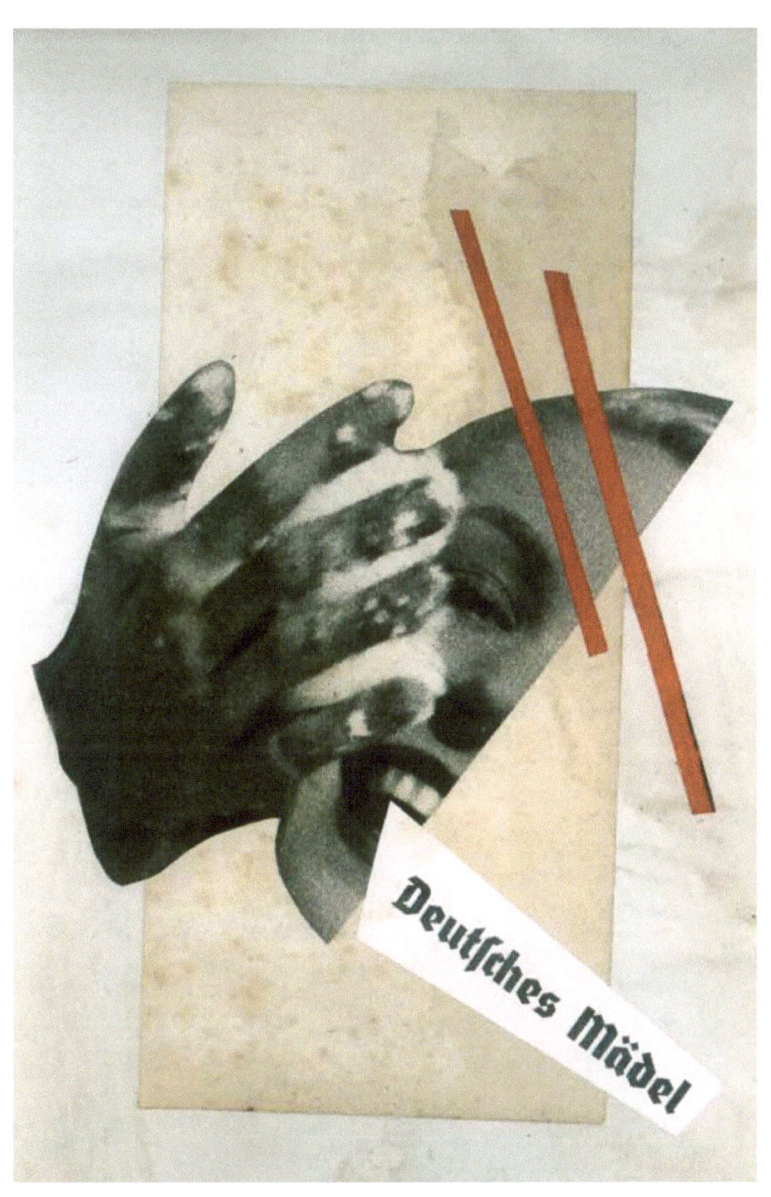

"This, then, is what counts: a lightning reaction which has no further need of conscious observation. In this respect at least the pupil makes himself independent of all conscious purpose."

Eugen Herrigel

cogarnaíl bhuí
i measc na nduilleog—
bréagaisnéis á scaipeadh

yellow whispering
among leaves—
daily spread of disinformation

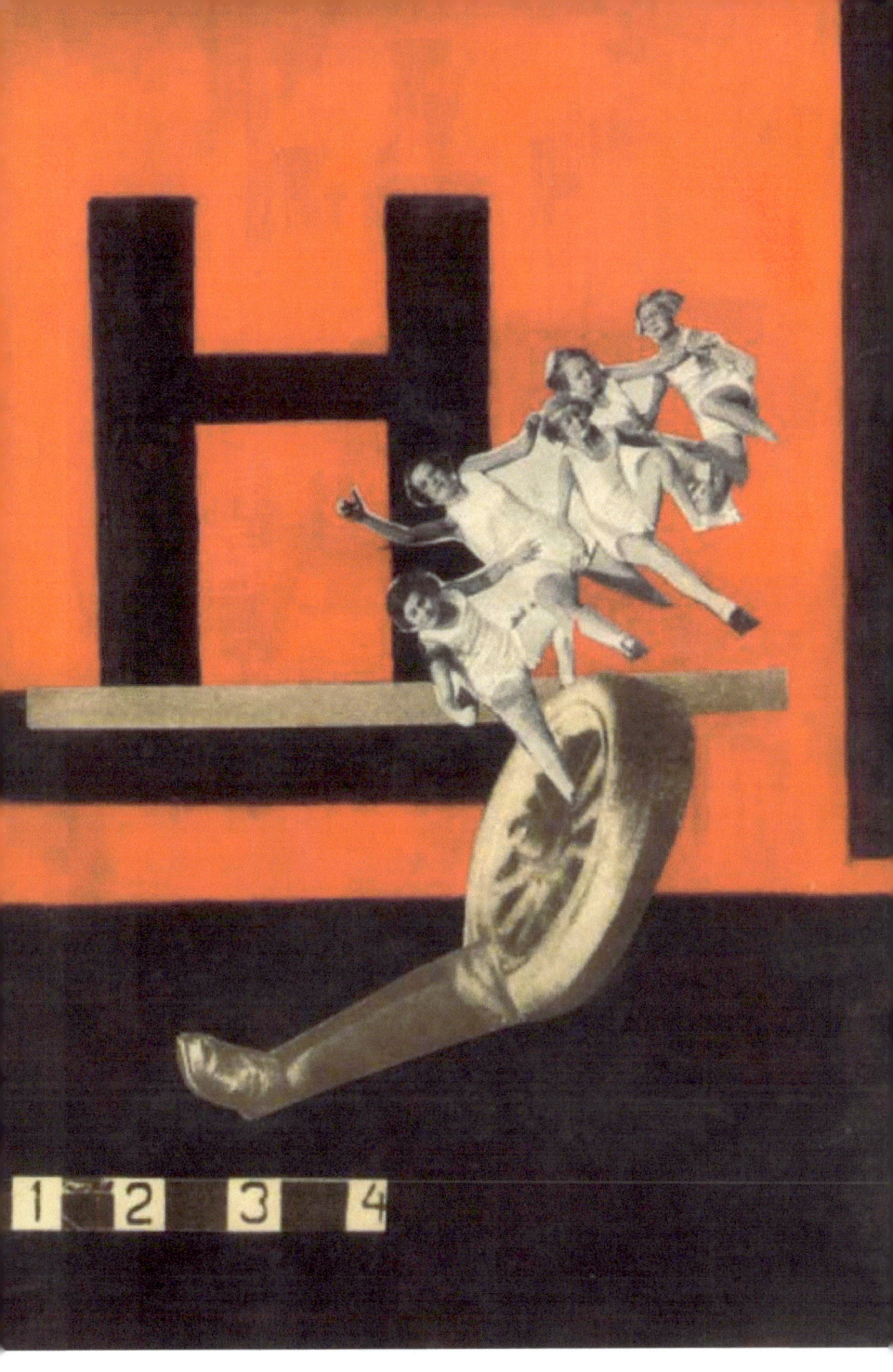

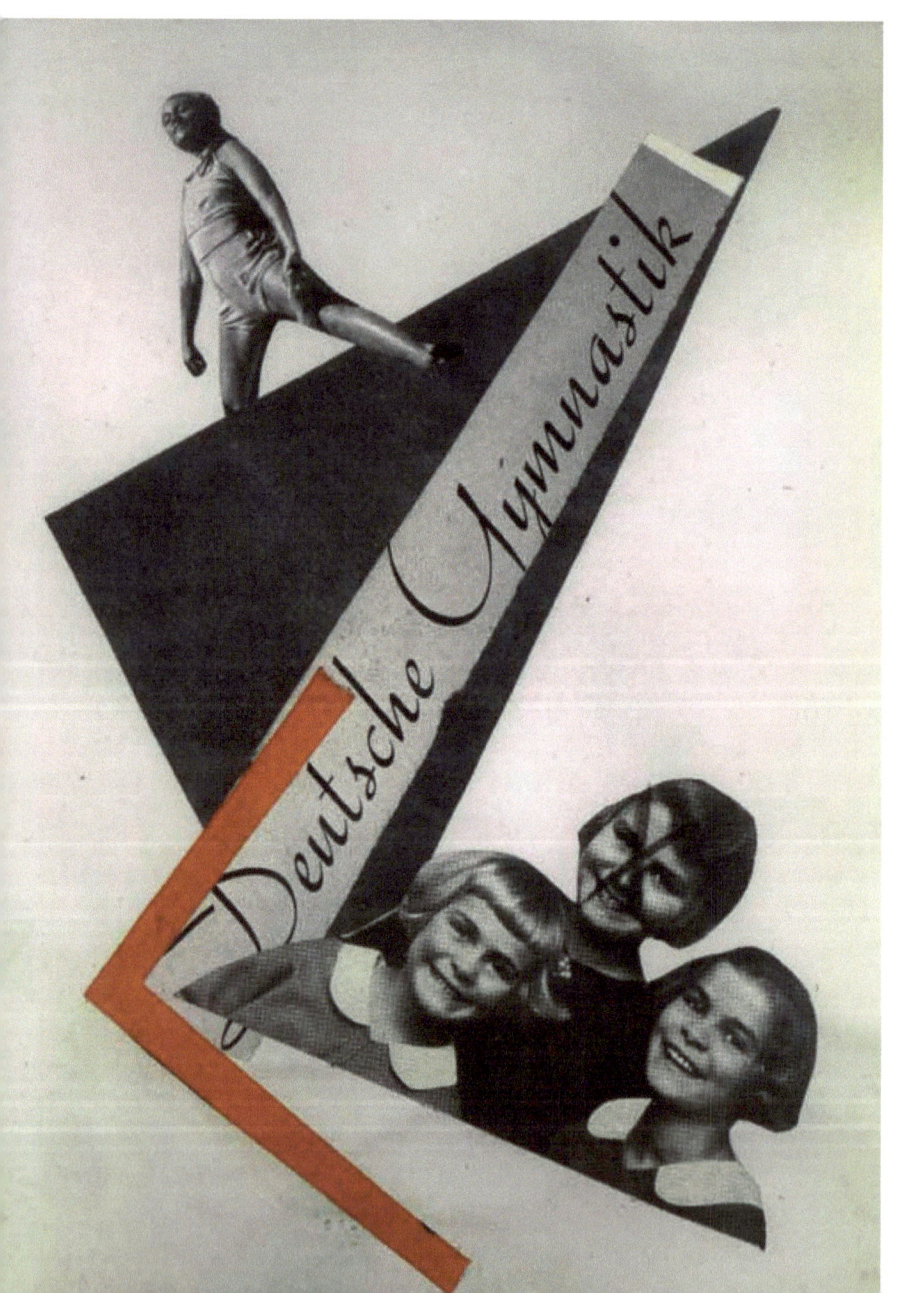

compánaigh ár n-óige . . .
cé acu atá i dteannta
na bpéisteanna

companions of our youth . . .
who among them is now
with the worms

what ever happens
to all the hats—
millions and millions of hats

cad a tharlaíonn
do na hataí go léir—
na céadta milliún acu

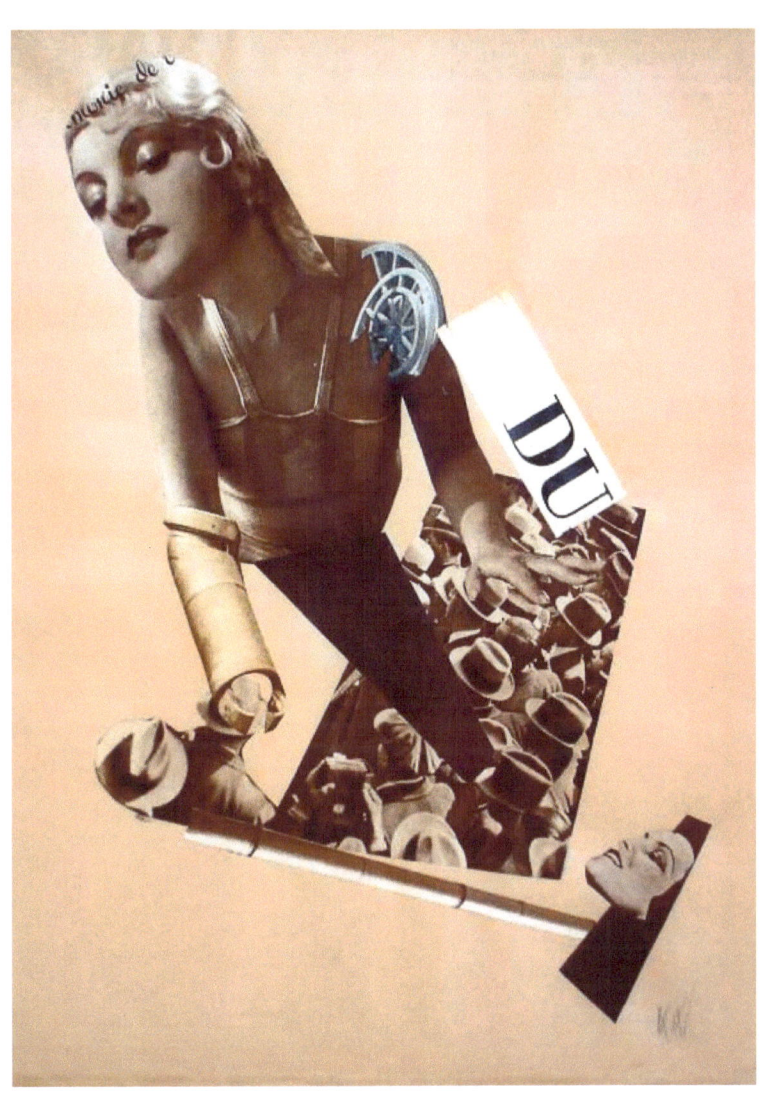

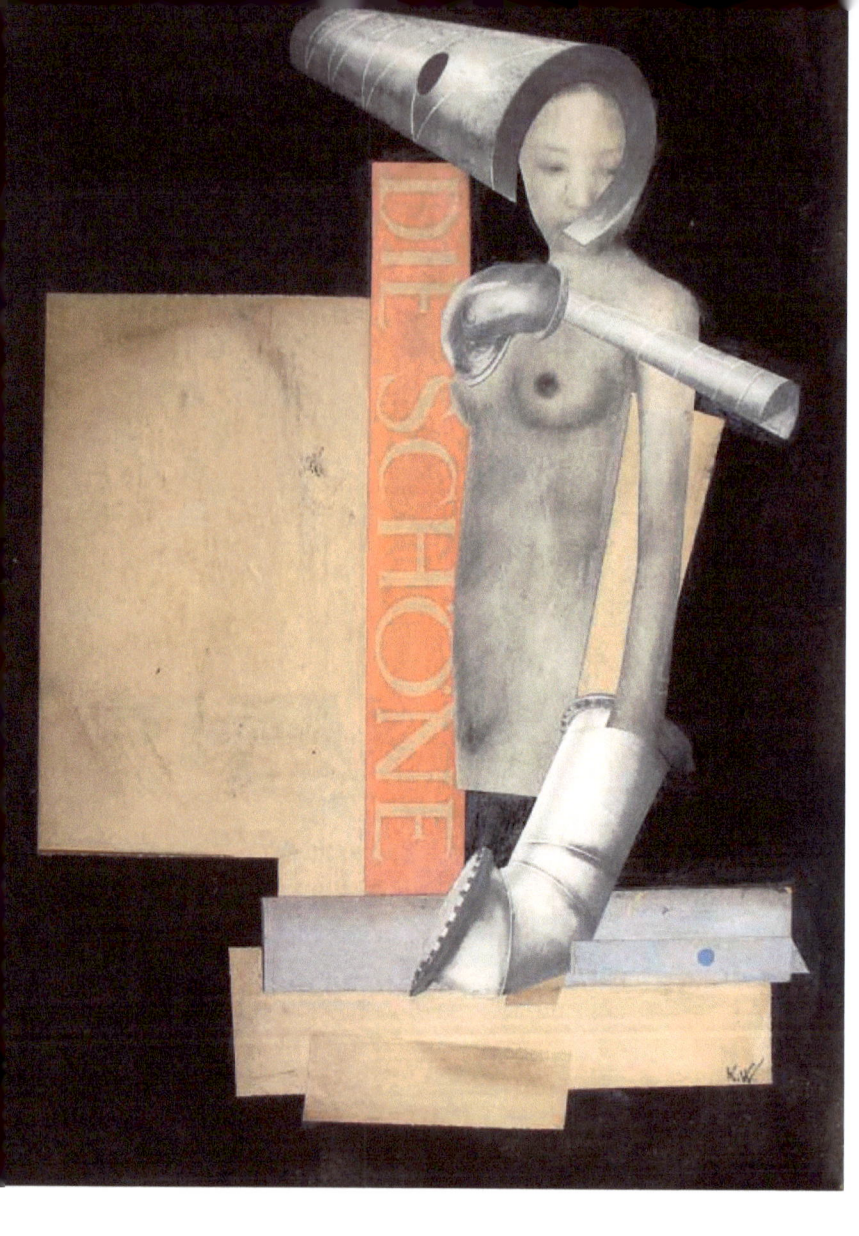

a dhuine chaoin
cá dtiocfainn
ar m'aingeal coimhdeachta

kind sir
where can i locate
my guardian angel

toirneach sna spéartha—
conas ár mbantracht
a chosaint ar bharbaraigh

thunder in the skies—
how to protect our womenfolk
from barbarians

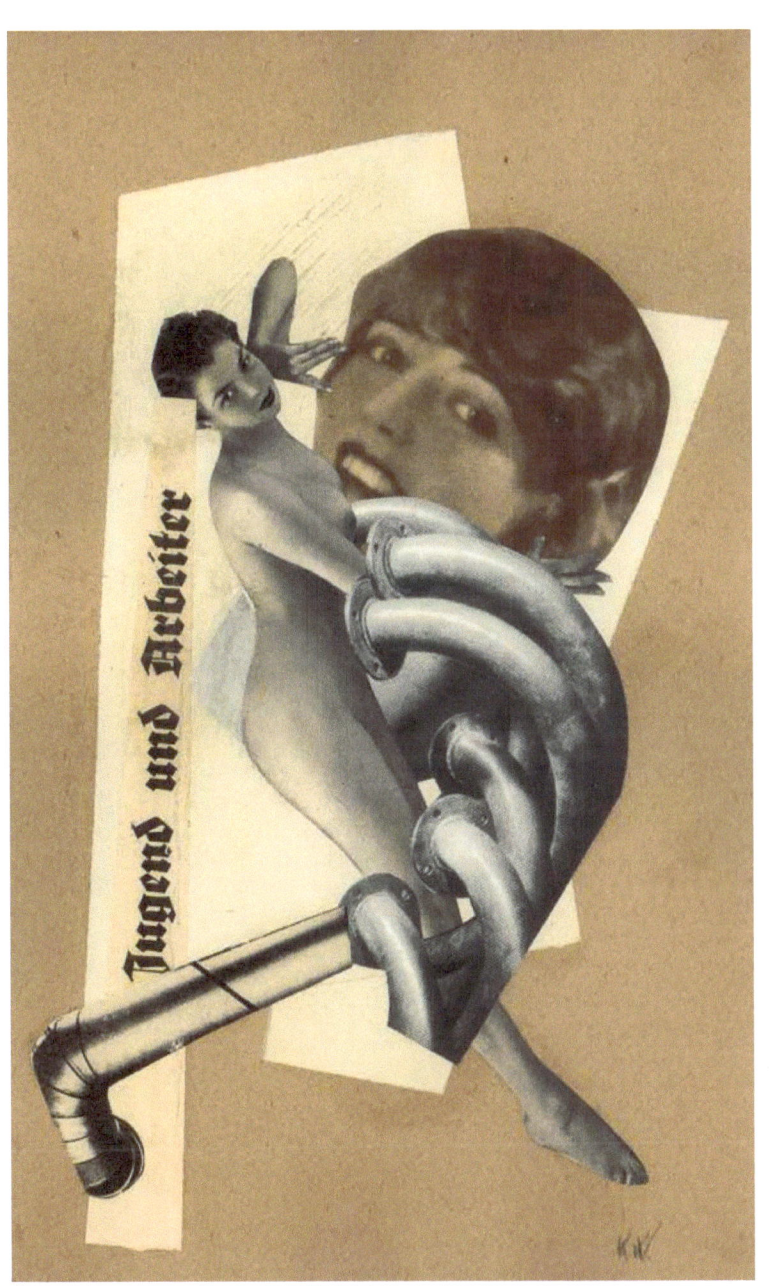

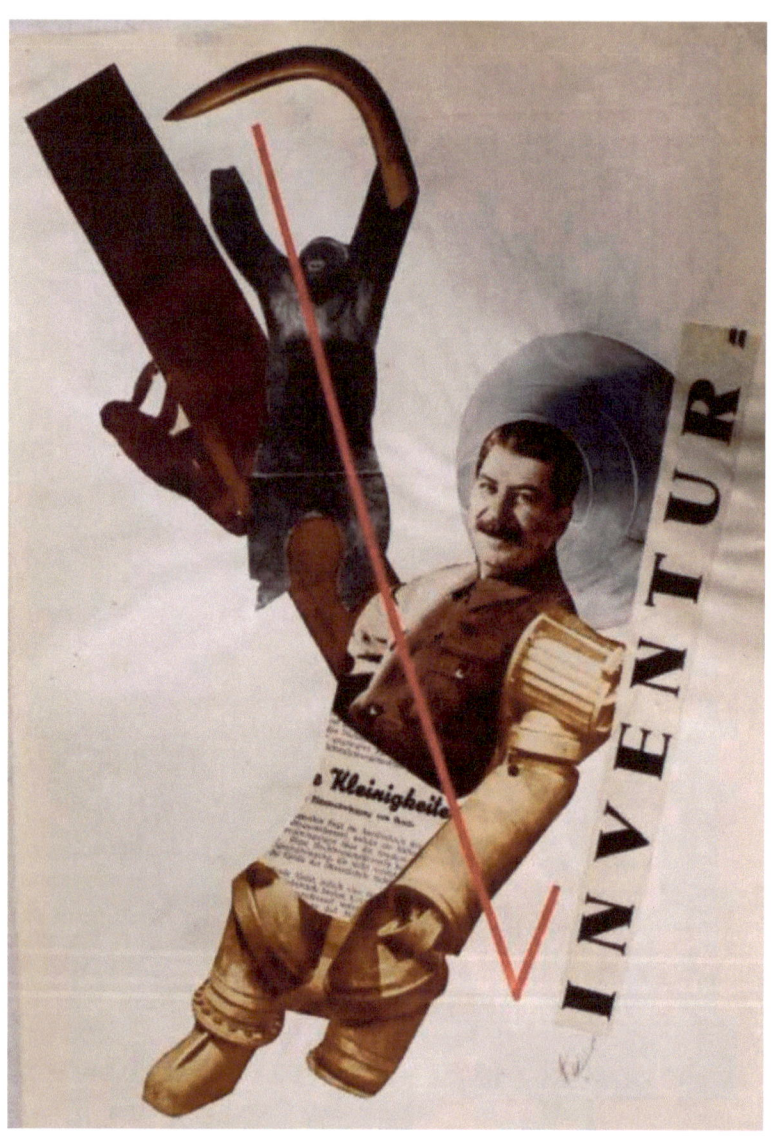

saol meidhreach—
saol dreancaide
i gcroiméal stailín

a jolly life—
the life of a flea
in stalin's moustache

lá ceobhránach—
fadhbanna cumarsáide
na cuaiche

misty day—
communication difficulties
of the cuckoo

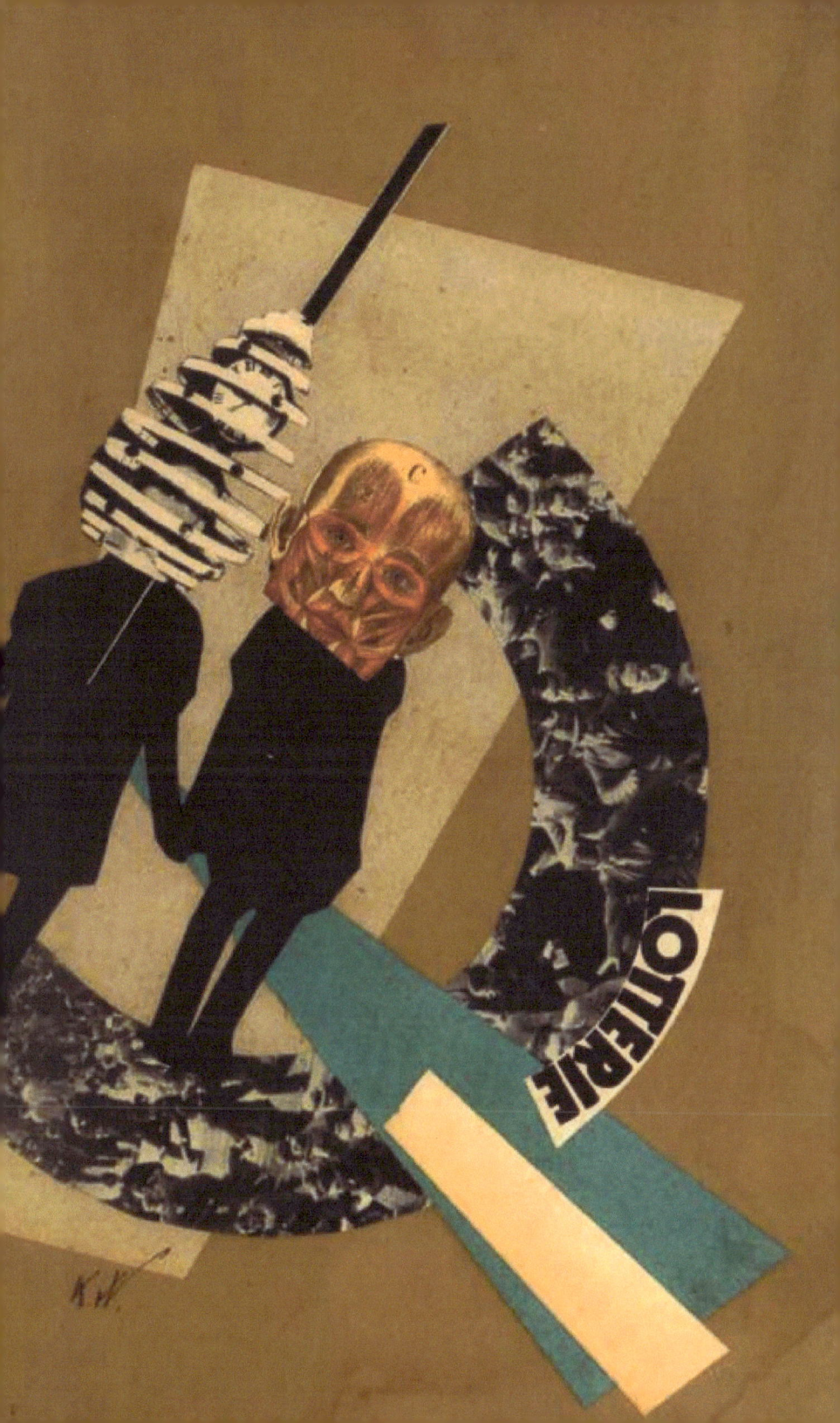

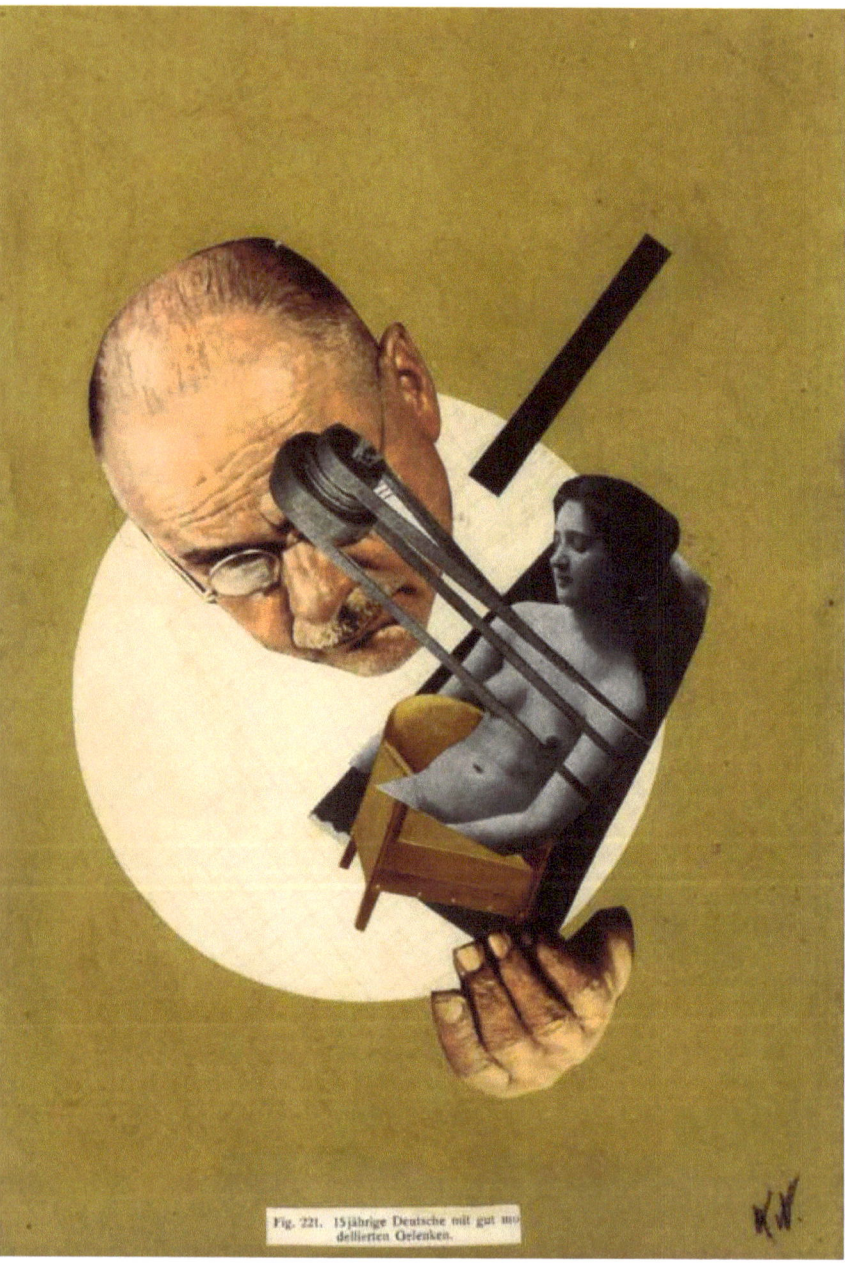

Fig. 221. 15jährige Deutsche mit gut mo
dellierten Gelenken.

an domhan ag athrú—
ealaín an bhasadóra
imithe i léig

changing world—
the art of the matchmaker
dying out

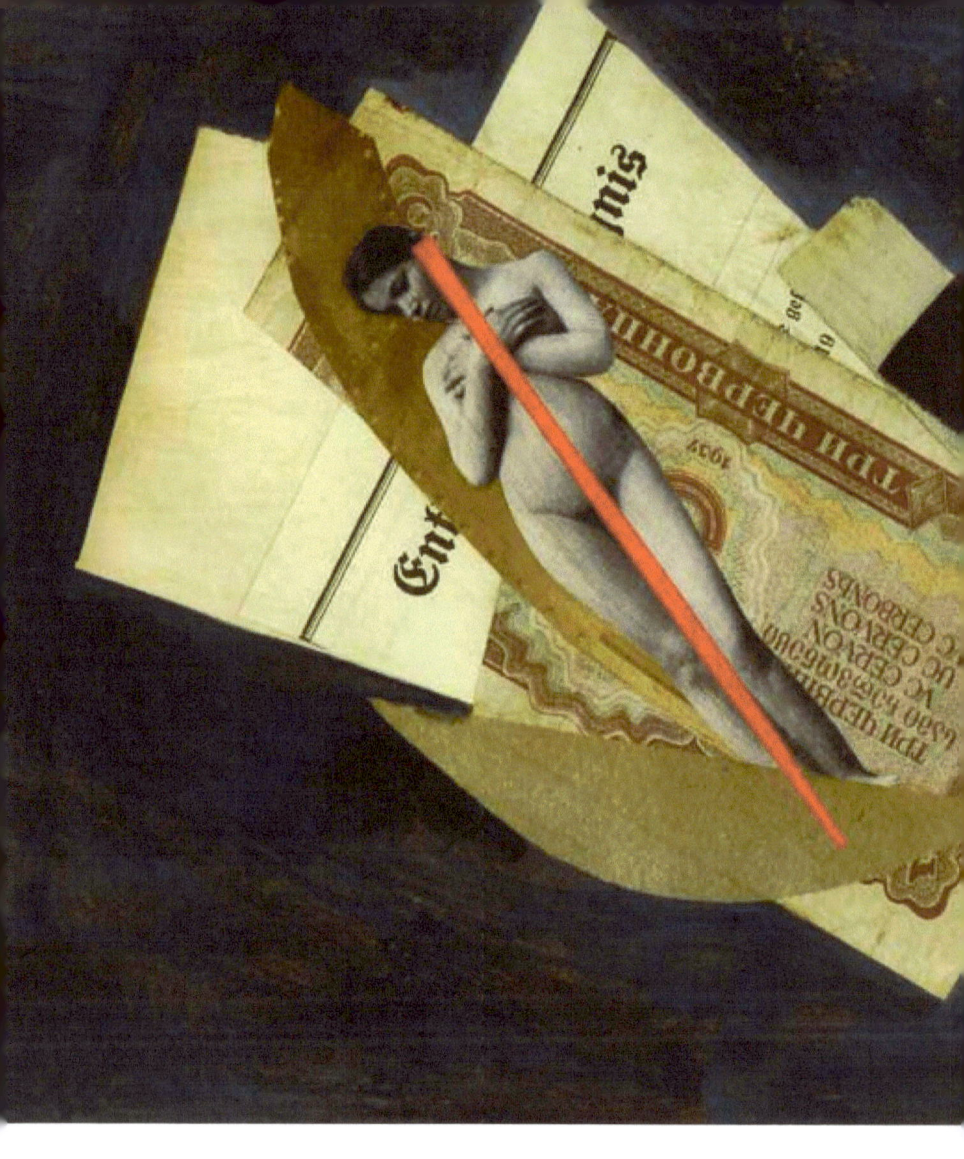

cén scéal
ag an bhfiliméala é—
'tá gach aon ní ar díol'

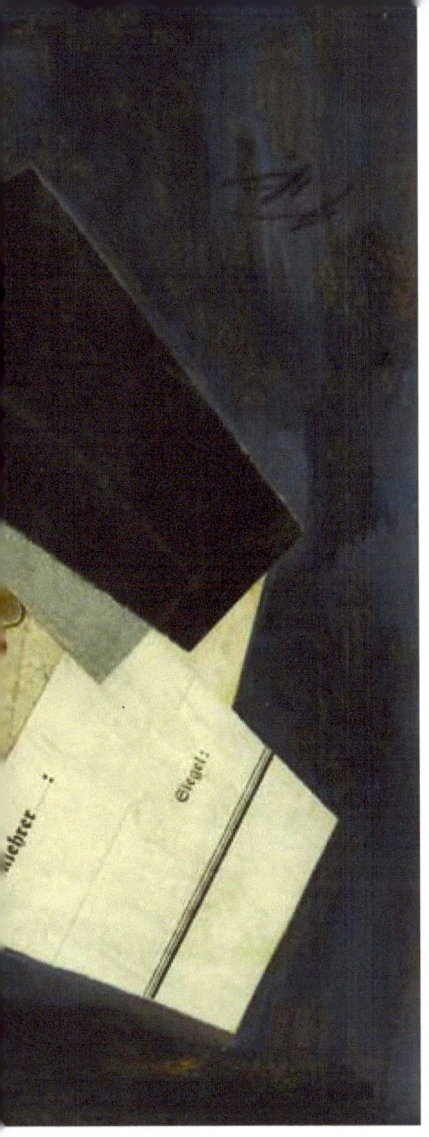

what is it
the nightingale sings—
'everything's for sale'

gaotha dána an mhárta—
soiprigh thú féin
a scallamáin

rude winds of march—
snuggle up
little nestling

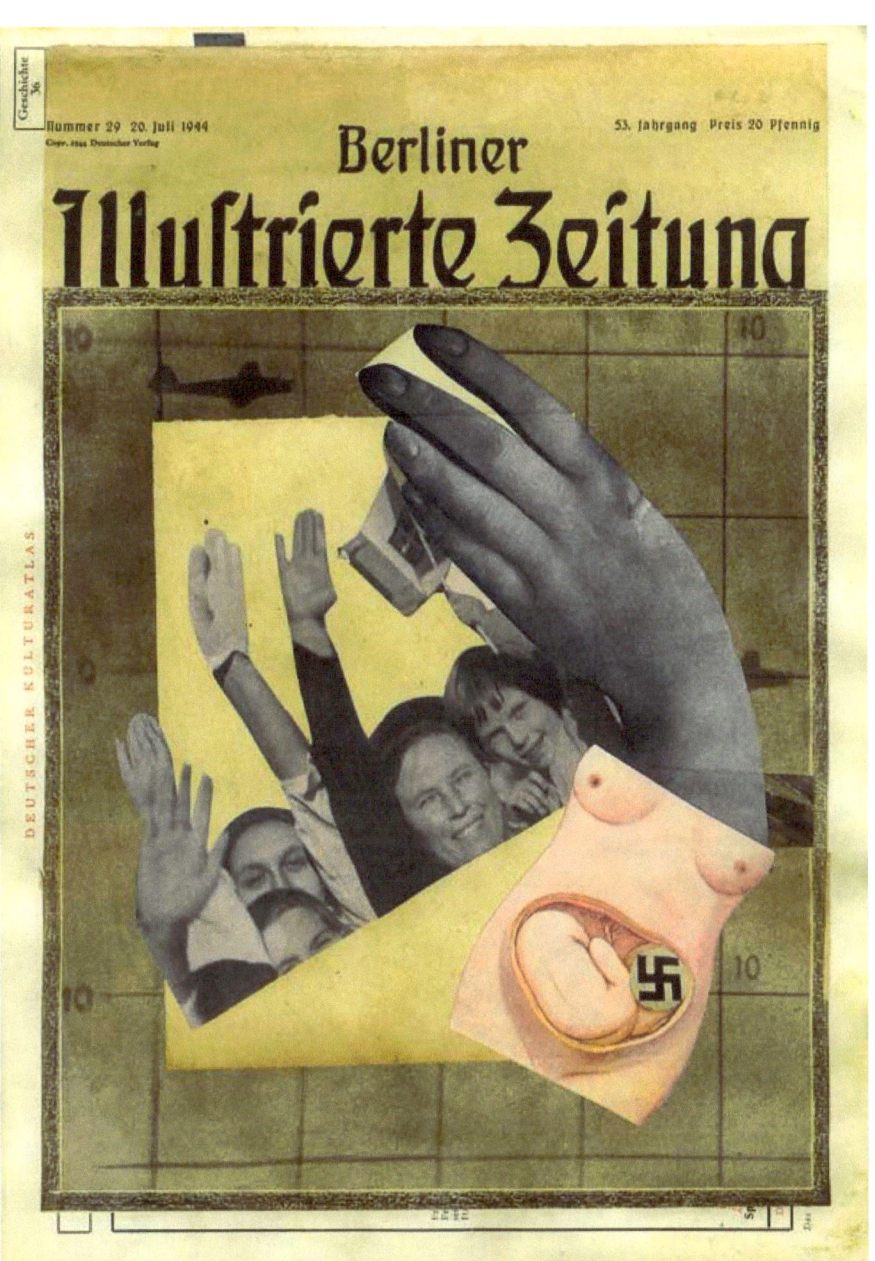

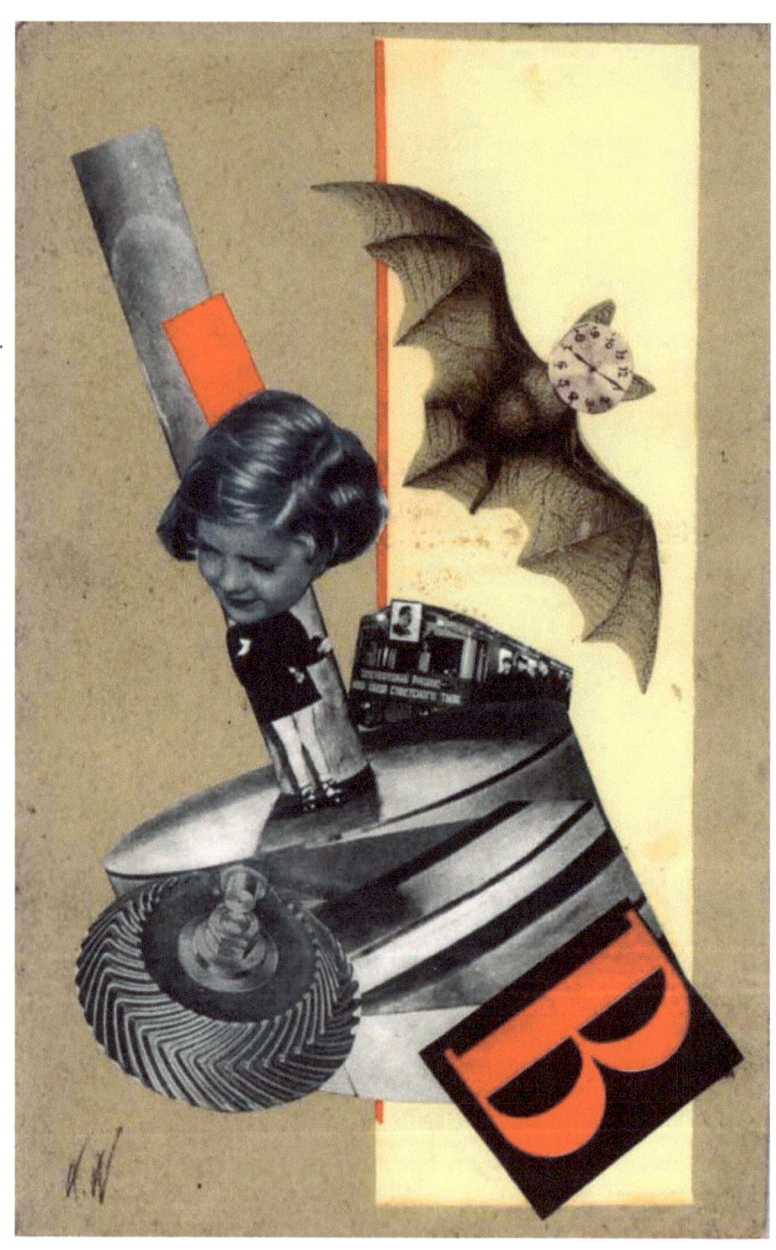

an t-am ar eite . . .
cén phluais dhorcha
atá ag feitheamh leis

time flies . . .
what dark cave
awaits it

tsvi nussbaum—
little nut tree
shaking in the wind

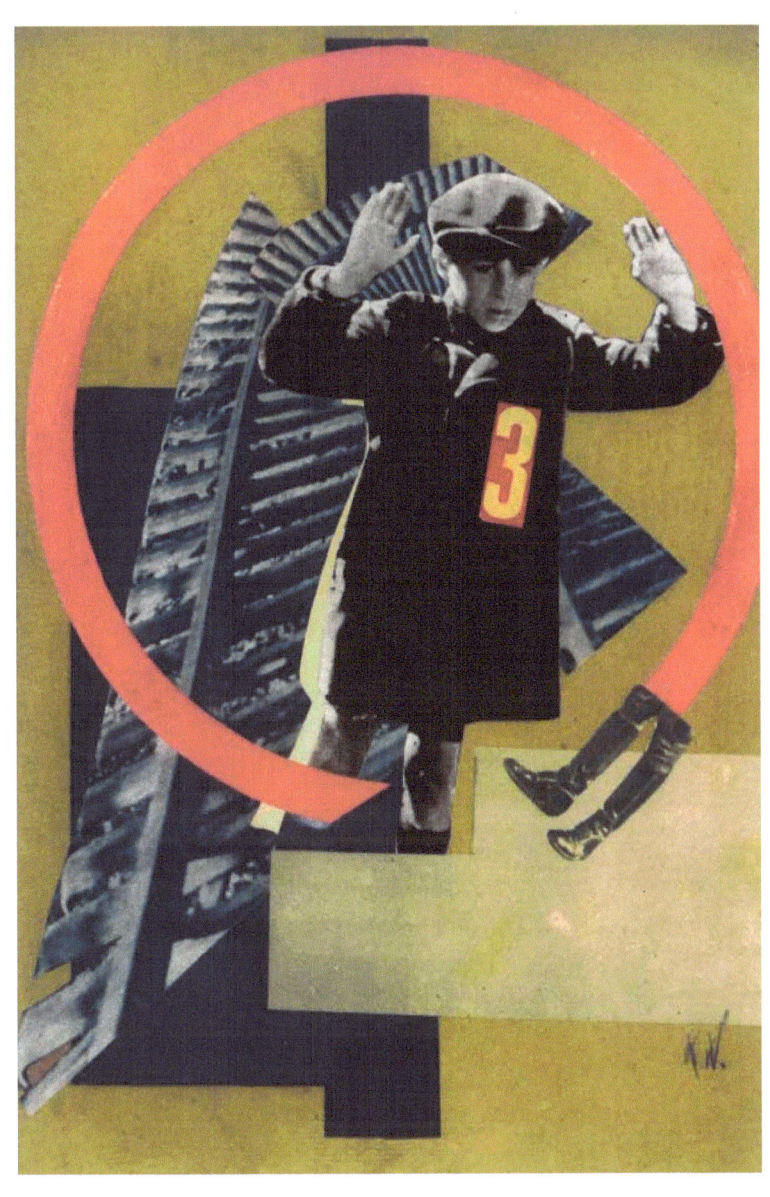

tsvi nussbaum—
crann cnónna beag
ar crith sa ghaoth

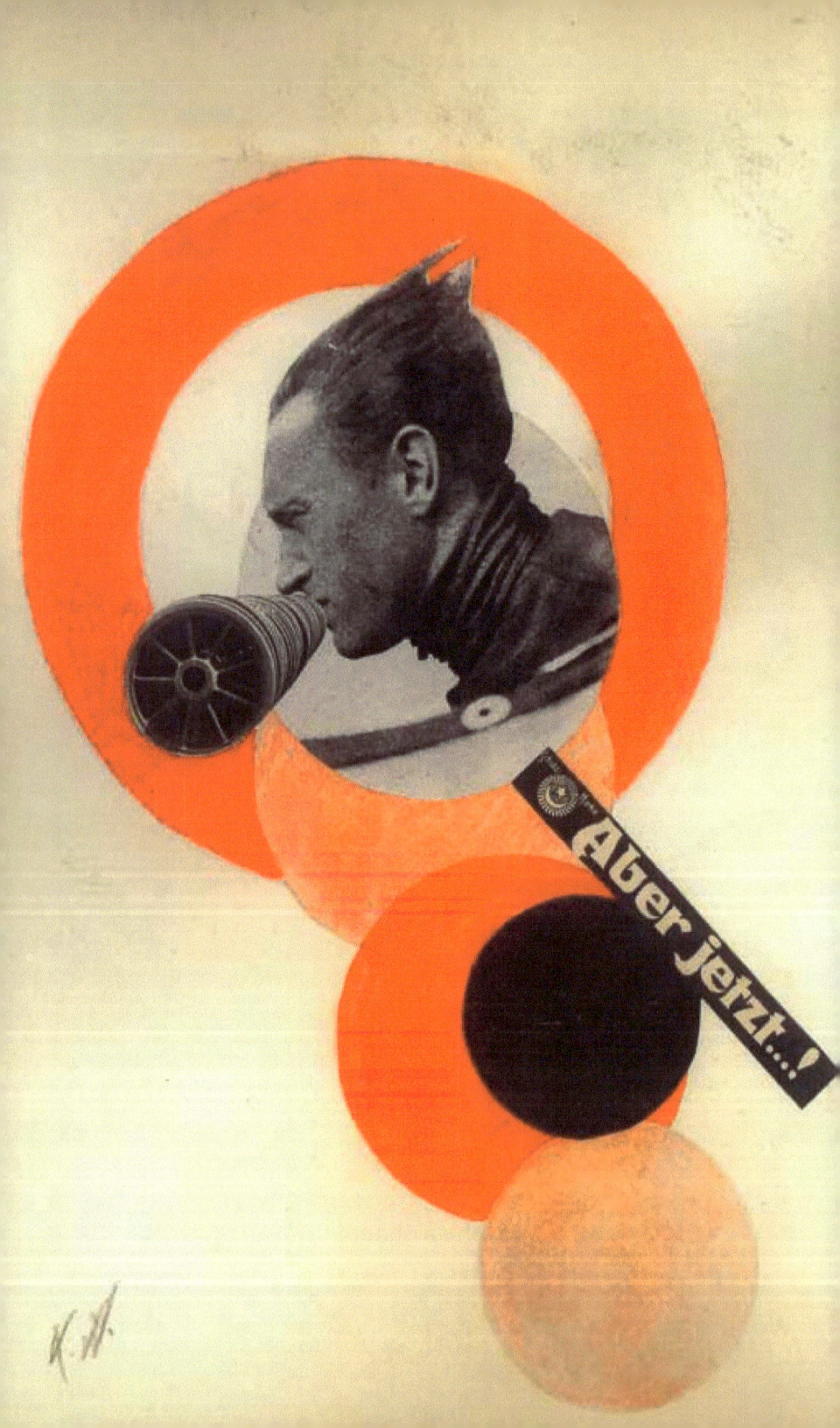

Aber jetzt...!

saorchaint
haiku saor in aisce do chách—
lon ar ghéag

free speech
free haiku for all—
blackbird on a bough

broidtráth—
tugaigí faoi deara lilí
an bháin

rush hour—
consider the lilies
of the field

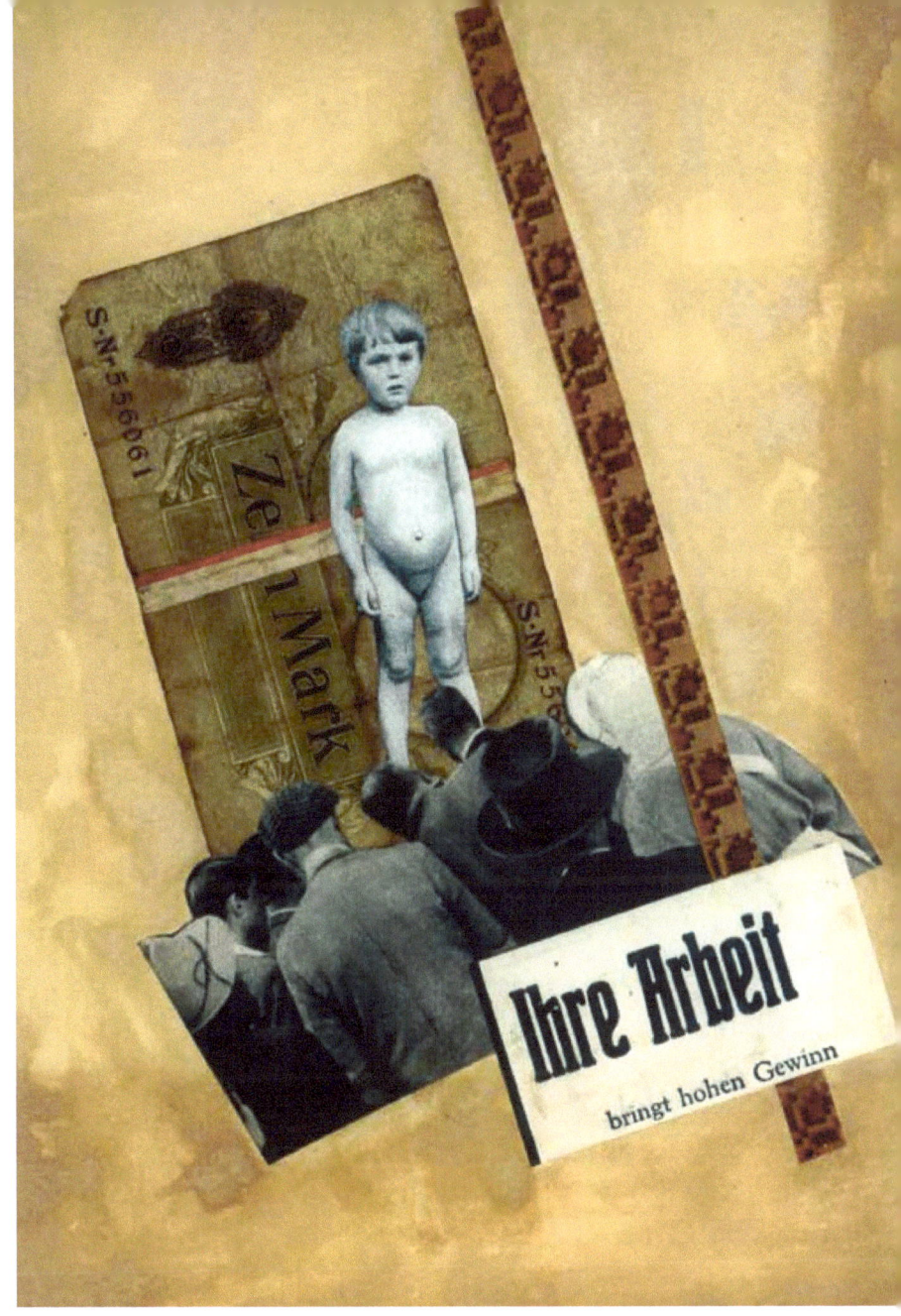

79

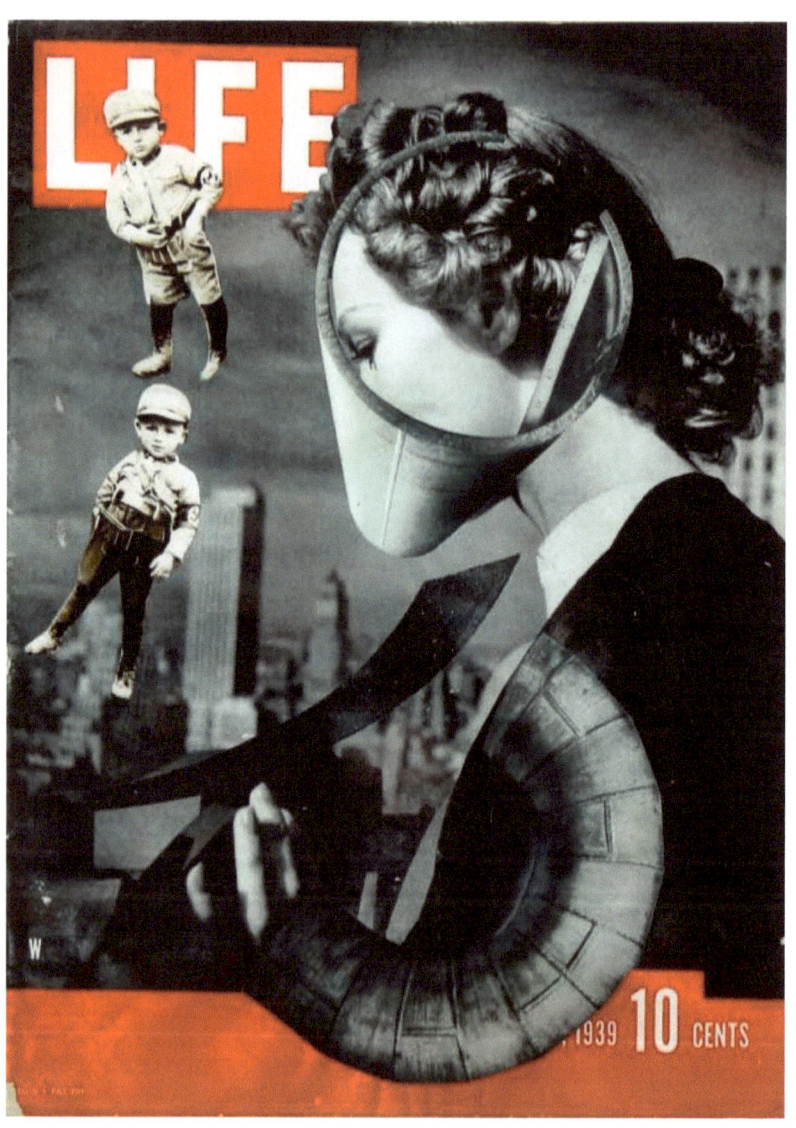

LIFE

1939 **10** CENTS

a dhuine chaoin
cén rud é an saol seo—
tabharfaidh mé deich cent duit!

kind sir
what is life—
i'll give you ten cents!

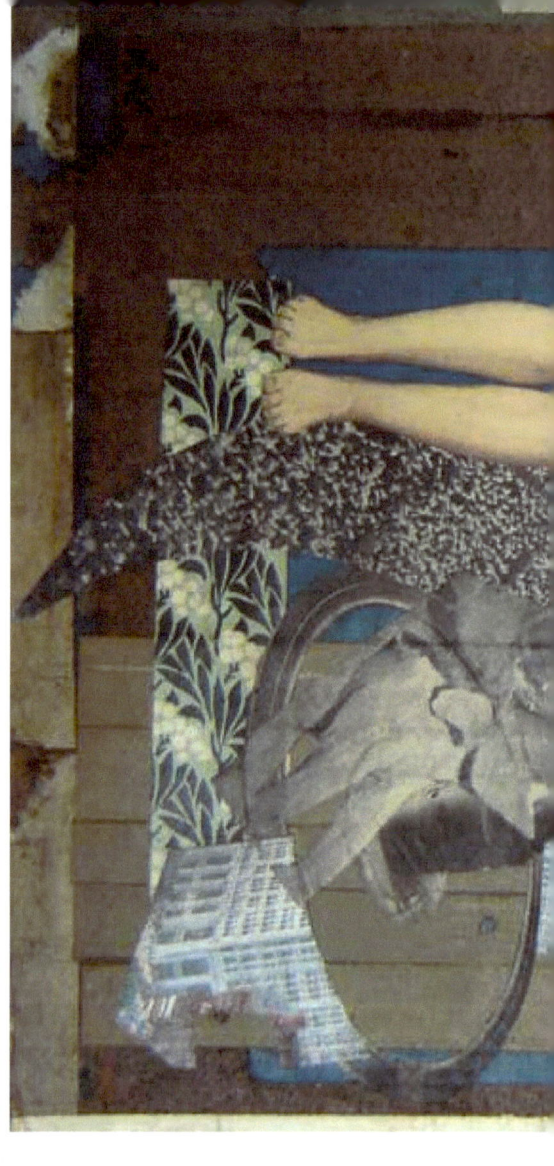

sé atá ann!
an cúcabarra i ngairdín
parthais

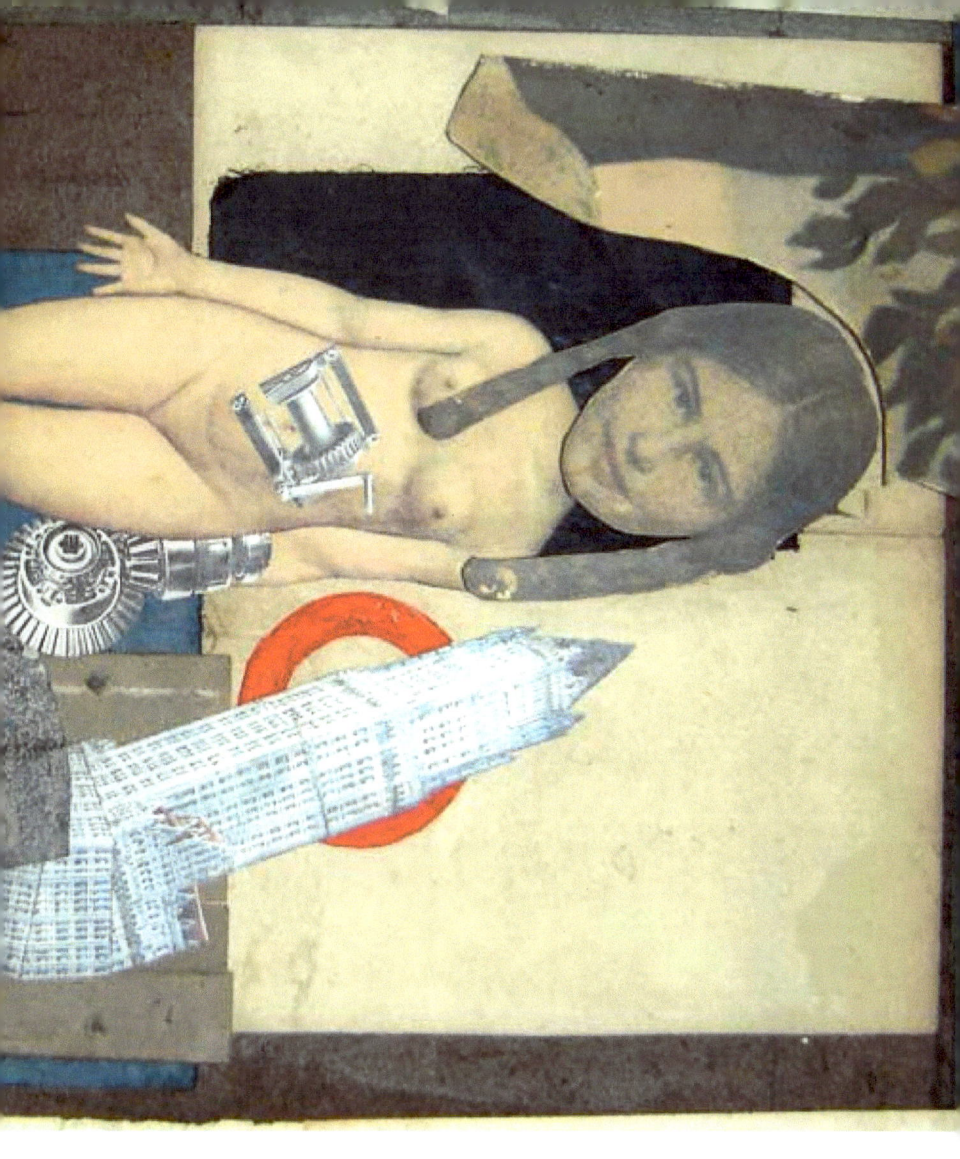

it is he!
the laughing jackass
in the garden of paradise

a dhuine chaoin
an bhfuil oifig phoist
thart anseo

kind sir
is there a post office
around here

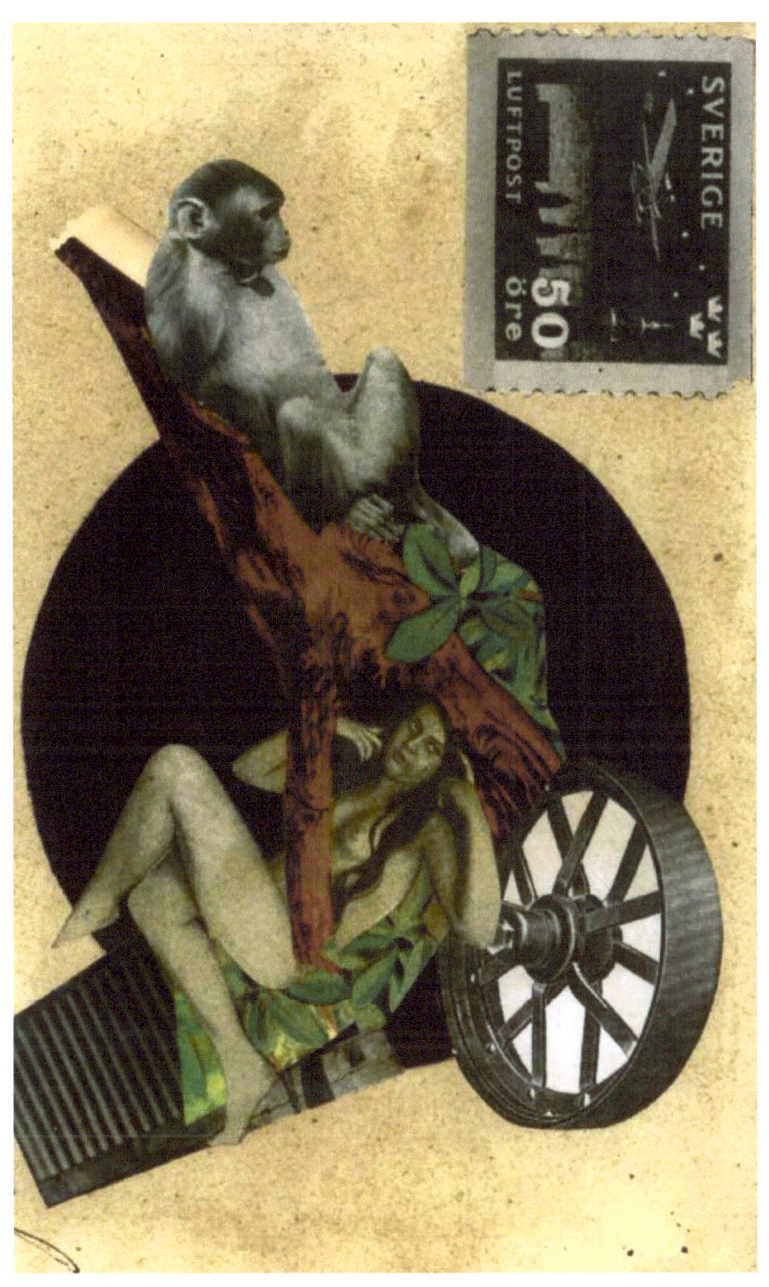

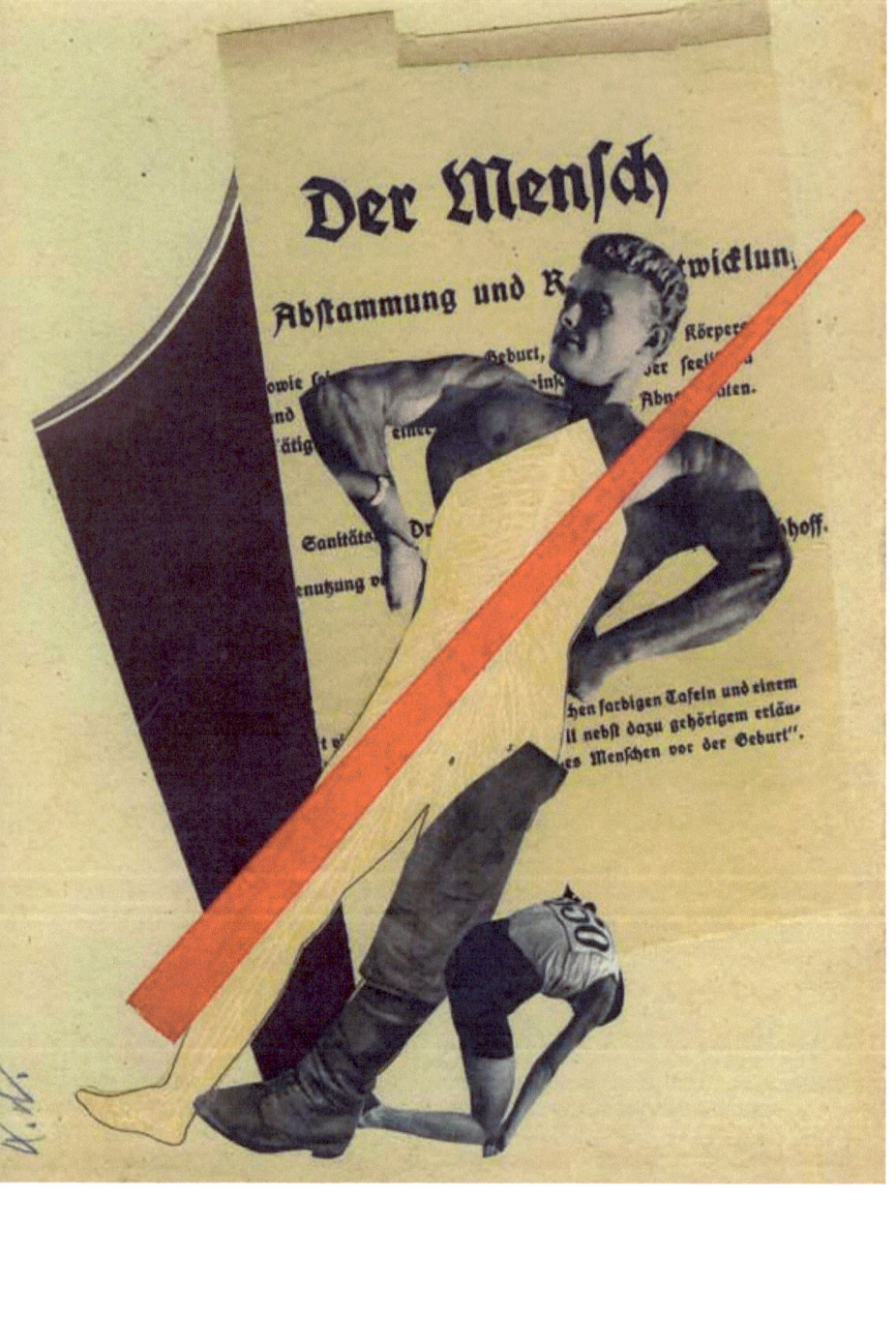

an aithneoimid é
an gcloisfimid inár dteanga féin é—
slánaitheoir

shall we know him
shall we hear him in our own tongue—
messiah

grág préacháin—
is mian lenár sinsir
labhairt linn

a crow squawks—
our ancestors wish
to speak to us

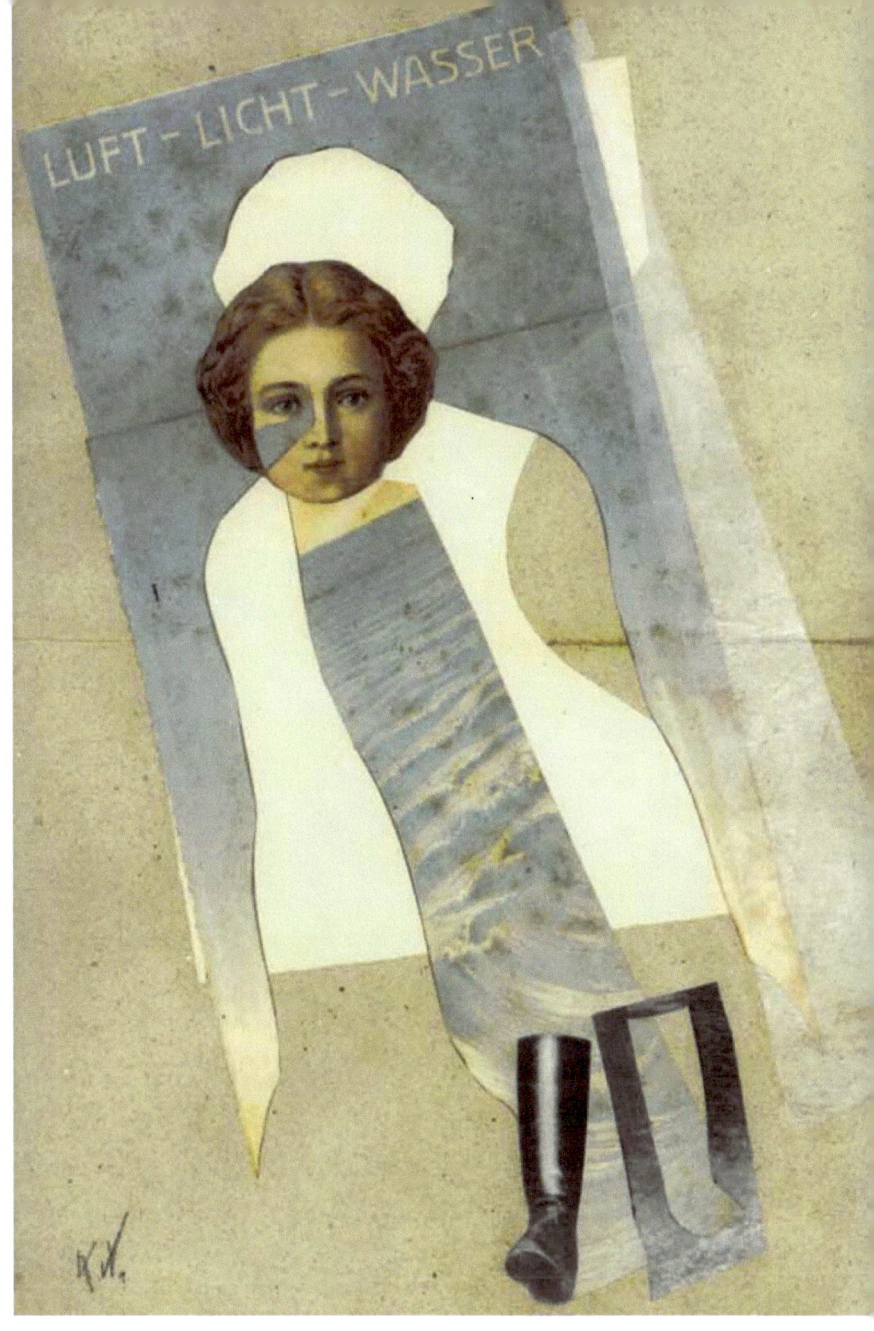

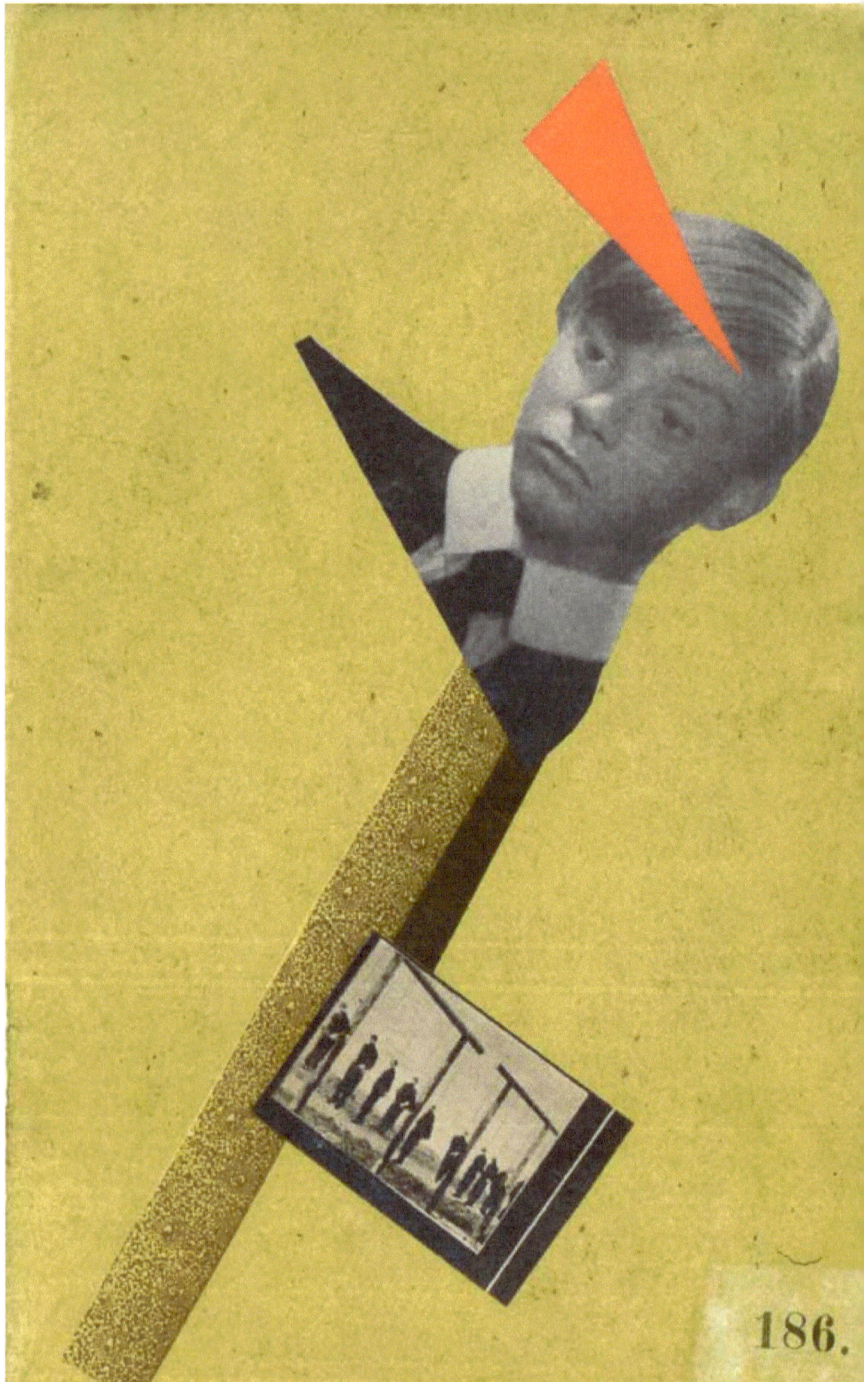

186.

a dhuine chaoin
ní mian liom crochadh thart anseo
níos mó

kind sir
i do not want to hang around here
any more

sean-lochán
léimeann frog ann . . .
báitear é

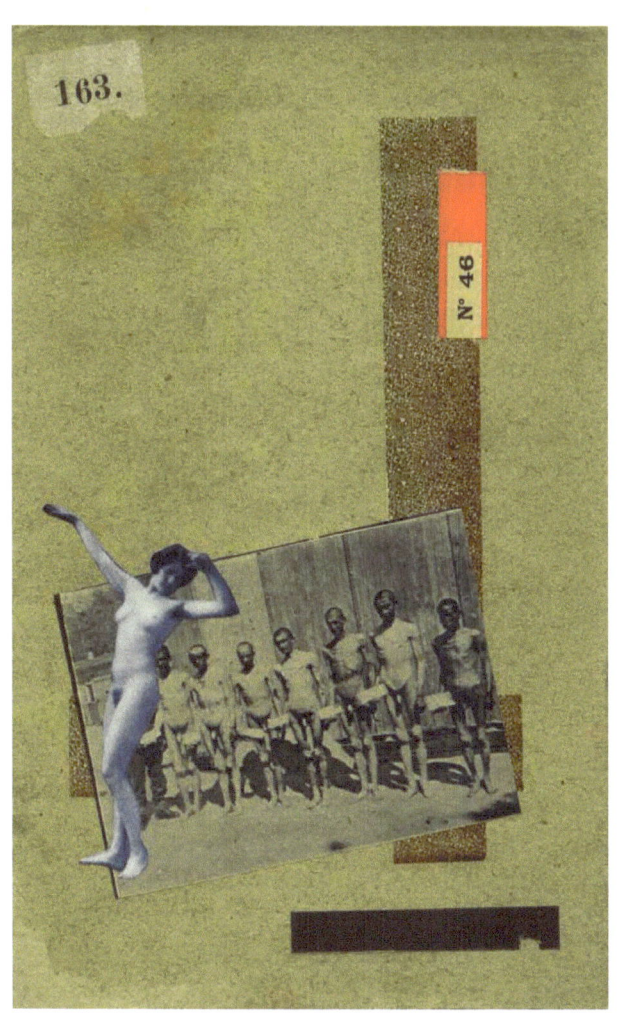

old pond
a frog jumps in . . .
and drowns

a dhuine chaoin
cá bhfuil hallaig
an fia gonta é an t-am

kind sir
where is hallaig
is time a wounded deer

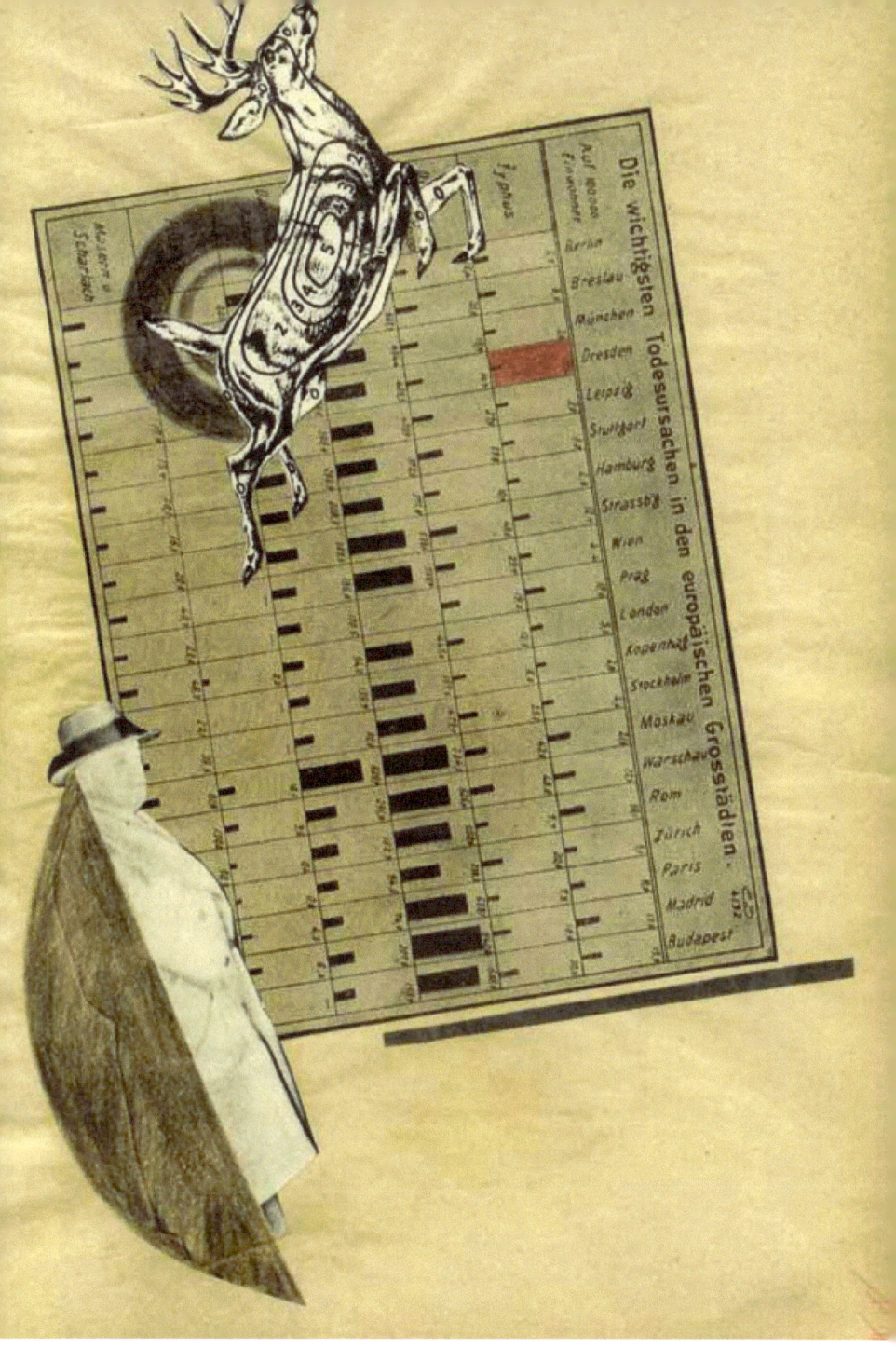

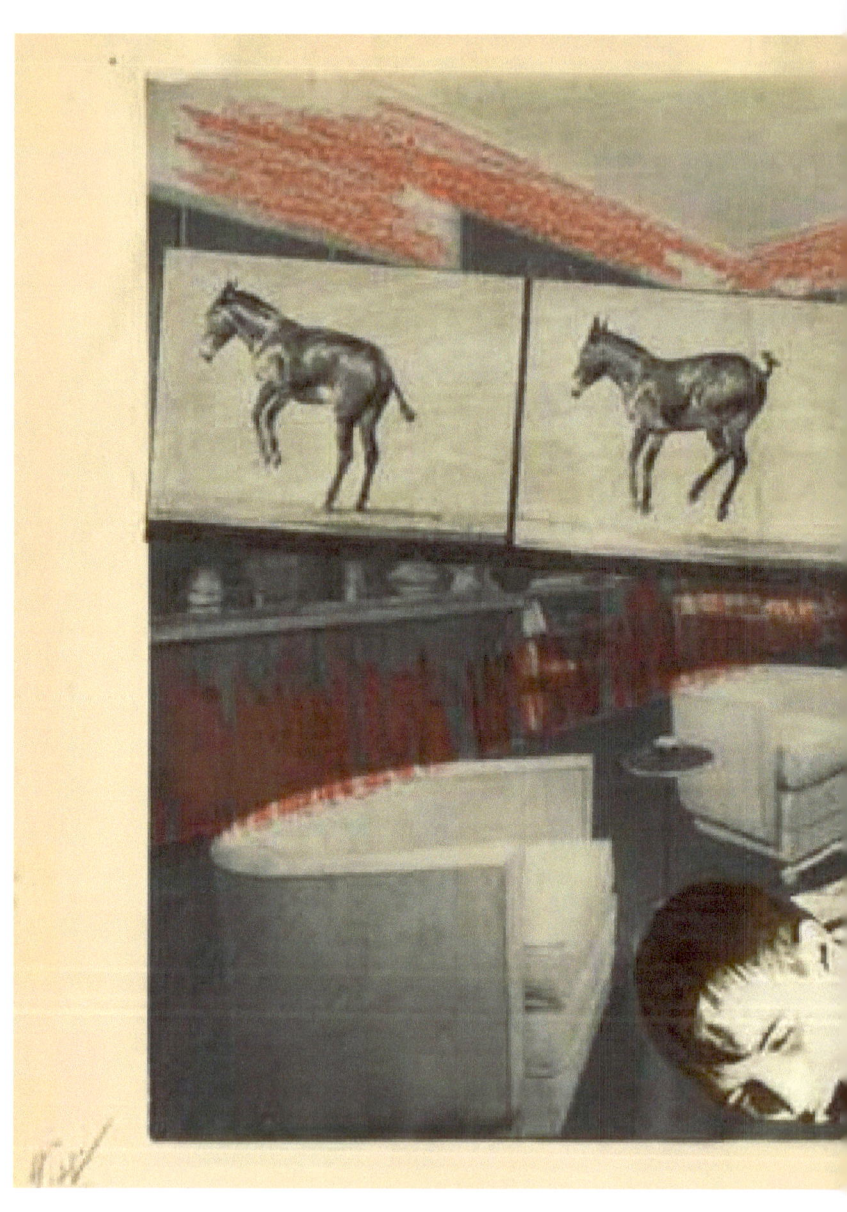

lá fhéile bríde—
guth an ghealbhain
go hiomlán nocht

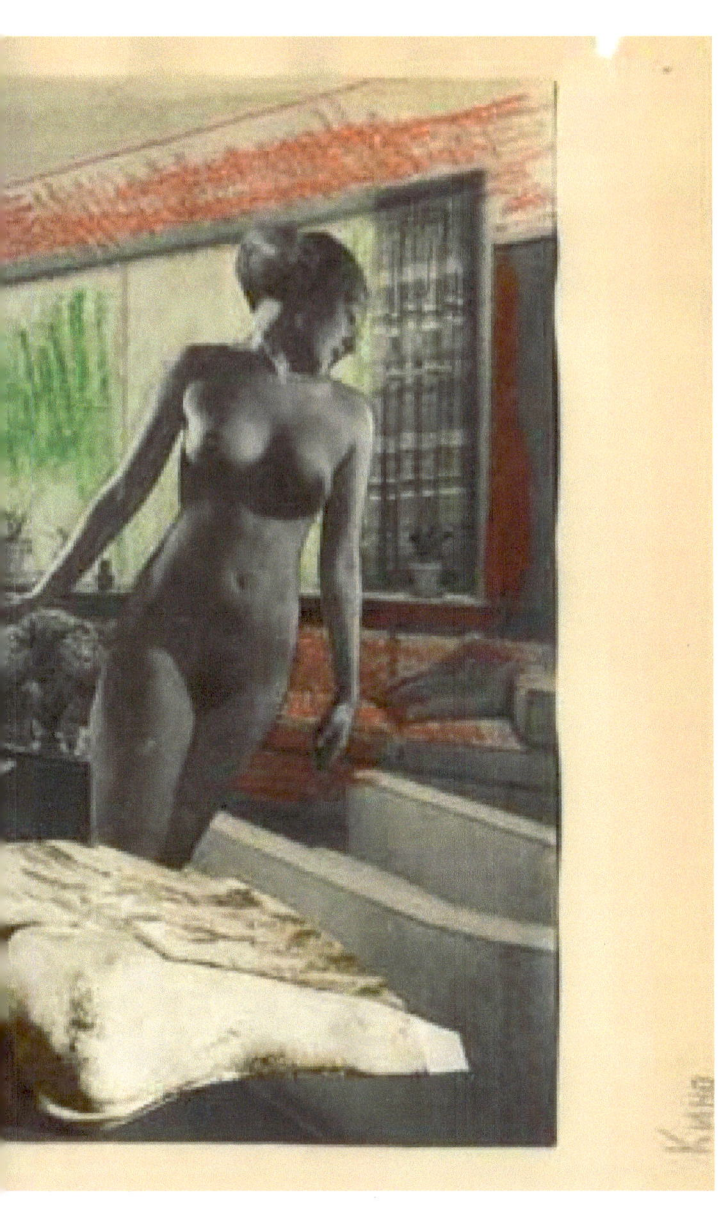

feast of st bridget—
the voice of the sparrow
completely naked

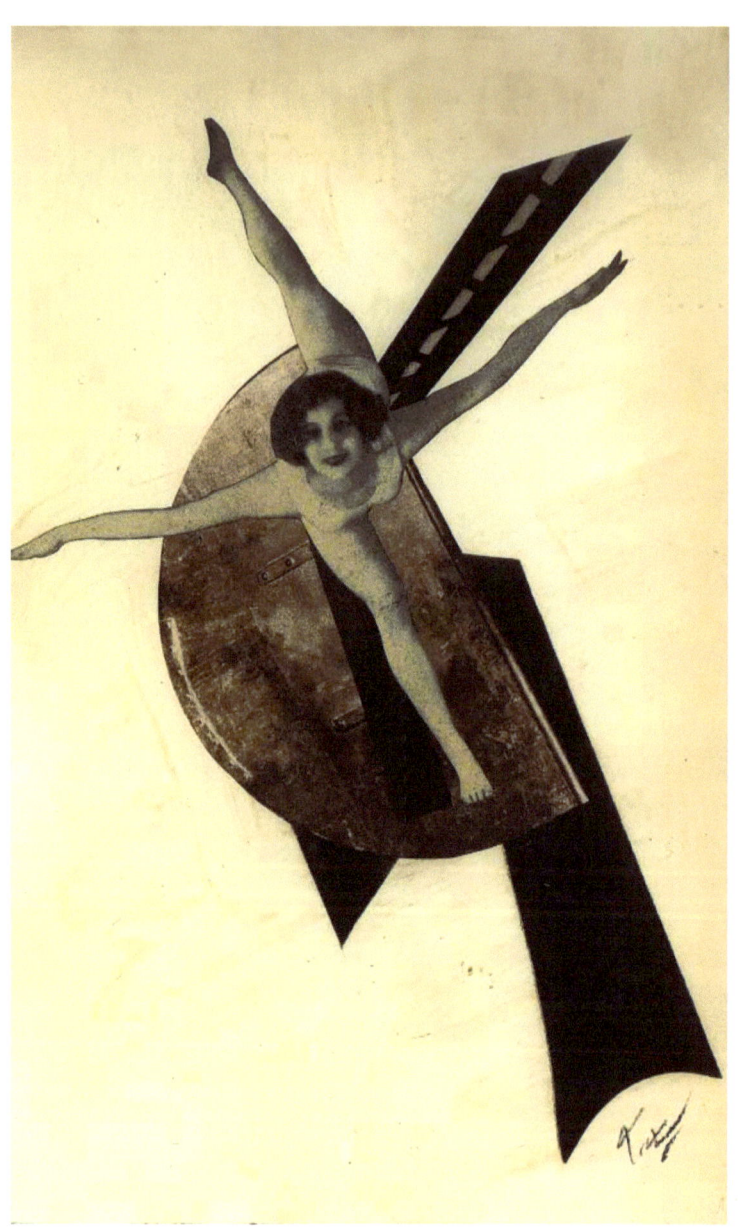

máithreacha
ar shnámhamar ina mbroinn—
a dhuine chaoin cá bhfuilid

mothers
in whose wombs we swam—
kind sir where are all my mothers

a dhuine chaoin
cén treo le do thoil
go dtí an t-oileán úr

kind sir
which way please
to the new world

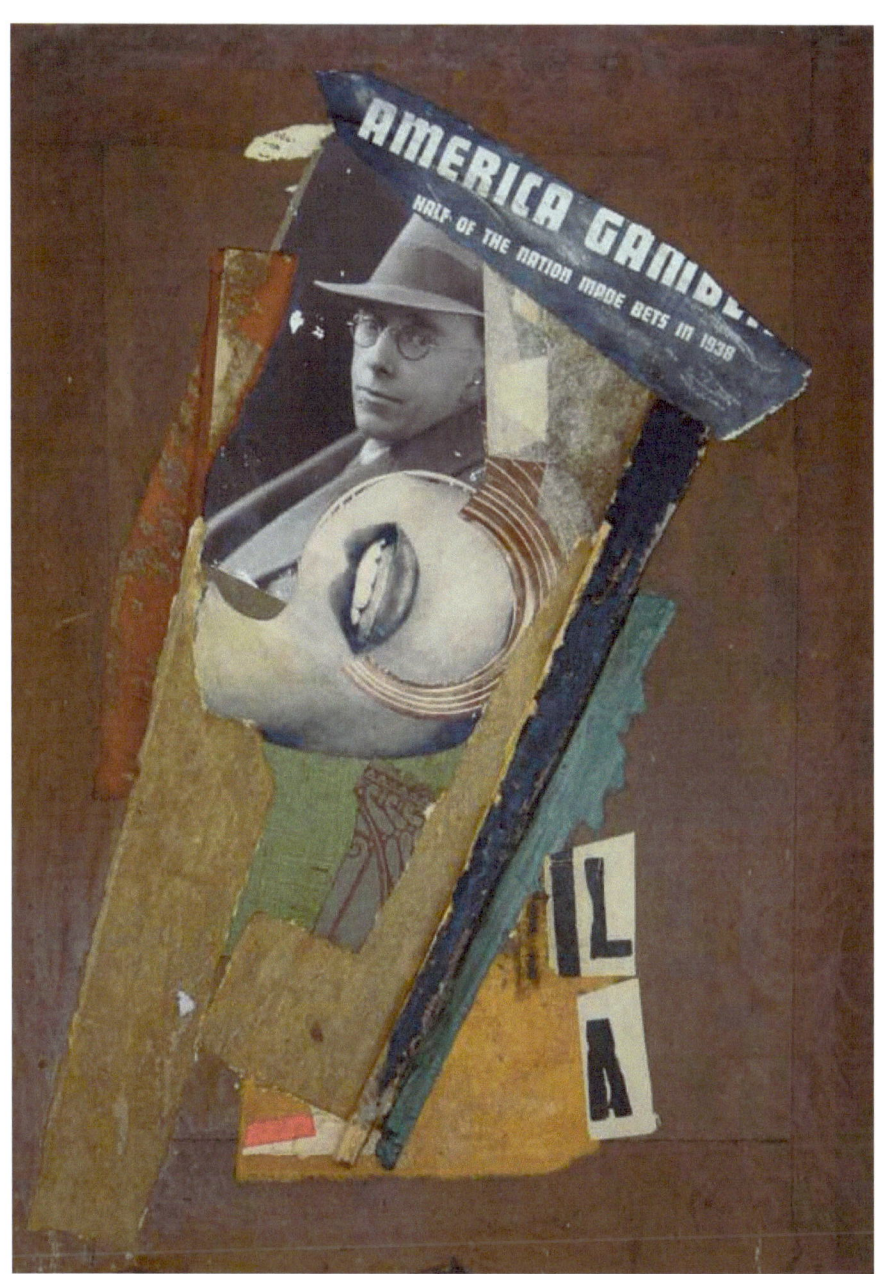

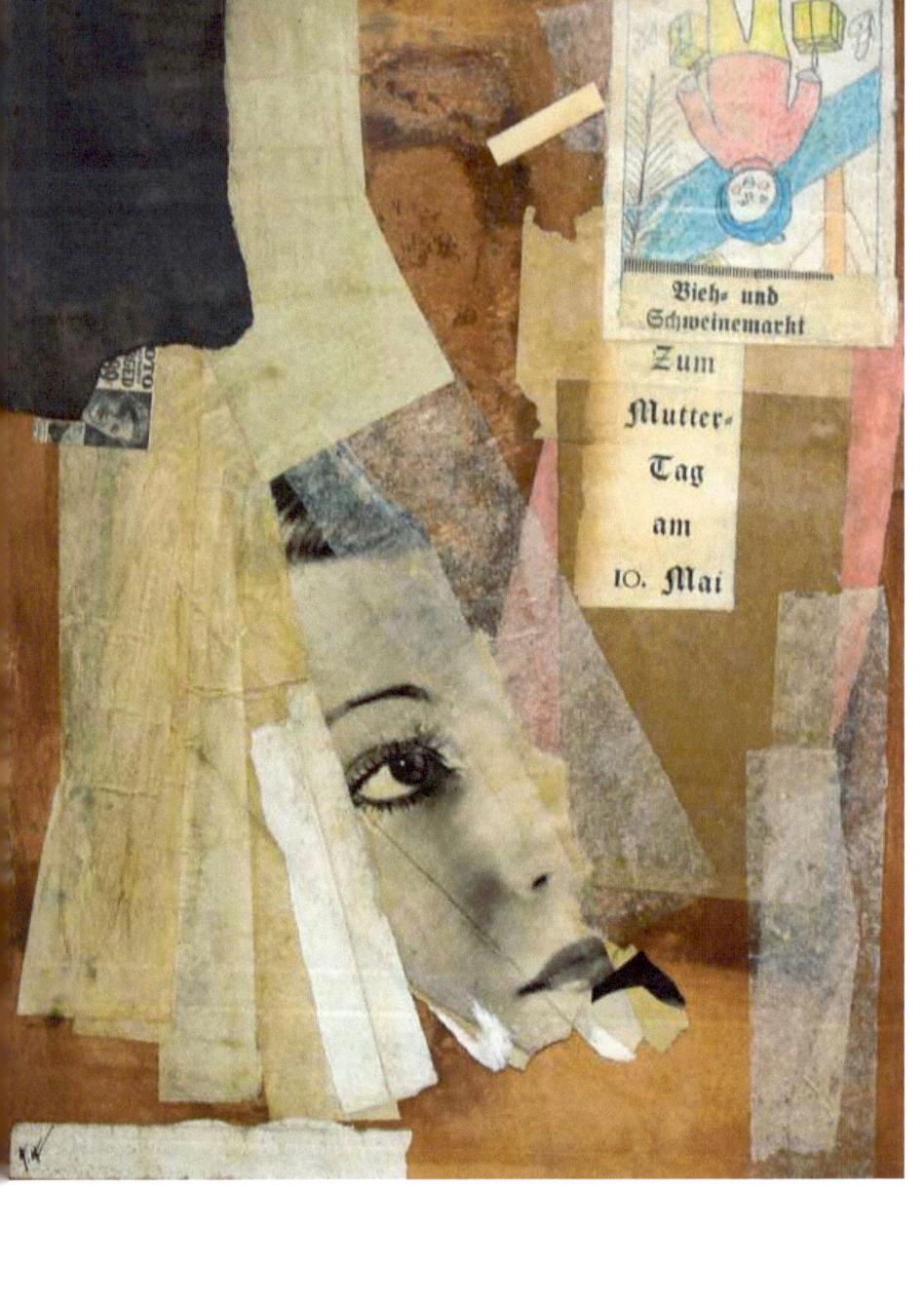

lá na máithreacha—
cadhain aonair
sa spéir

mothers' day—
a lone goose
in the sky

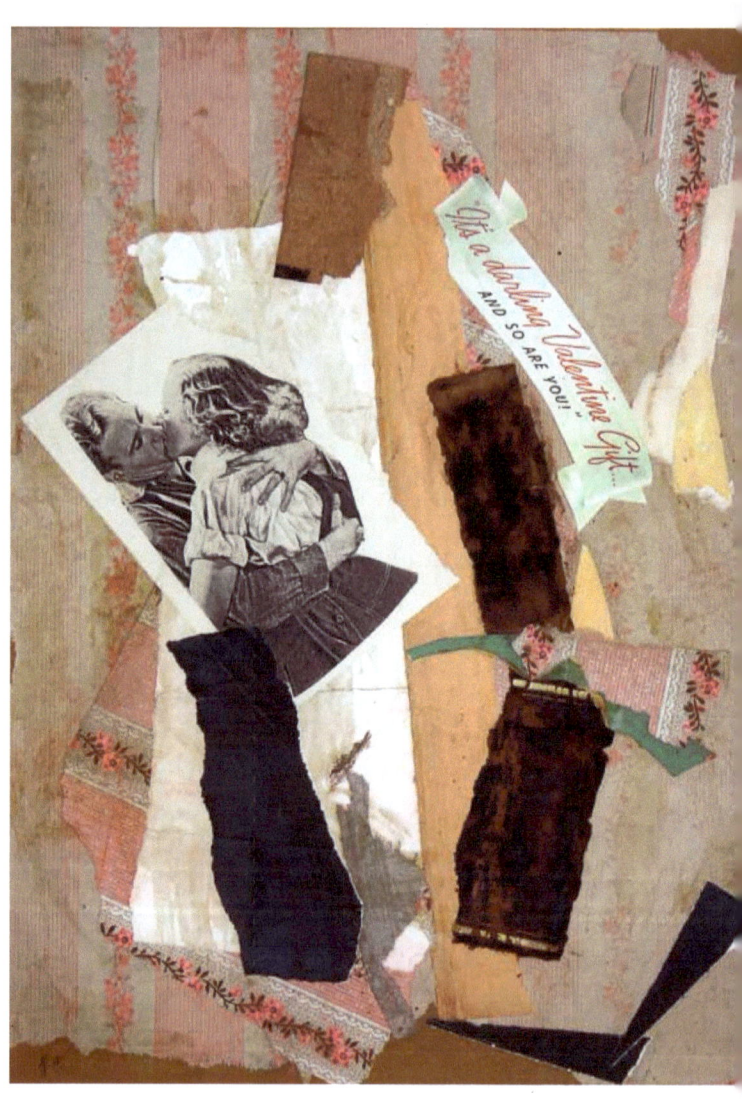

glór crotaigh
sa chontráth—
póga dearmadta

curlew call
at dusk—
forgotten kisses

lilí
an bháin—
dreofaidh siadsan freisin

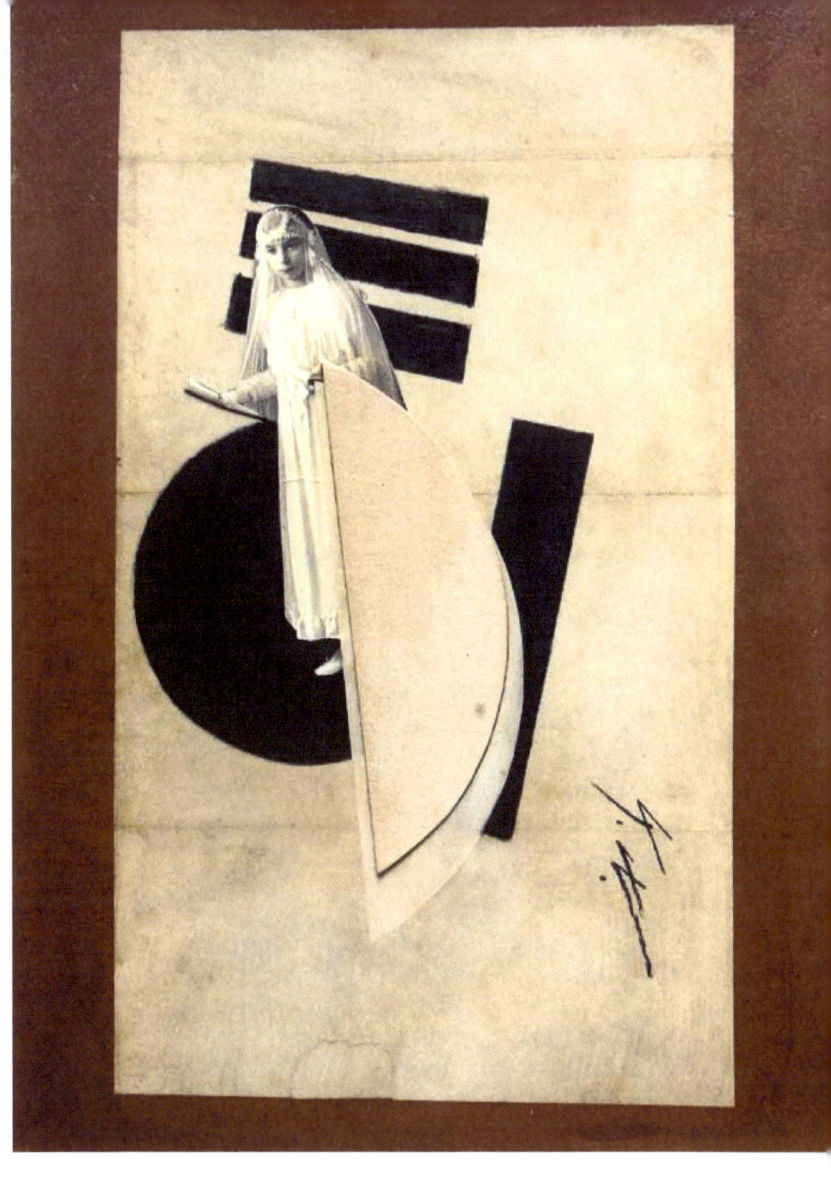

lilies
of the field—
they too must rot

lá fada
i ndeireadh thiar thall
an bhábóg ina codladh

a long day—
now at last
the doll's asleep

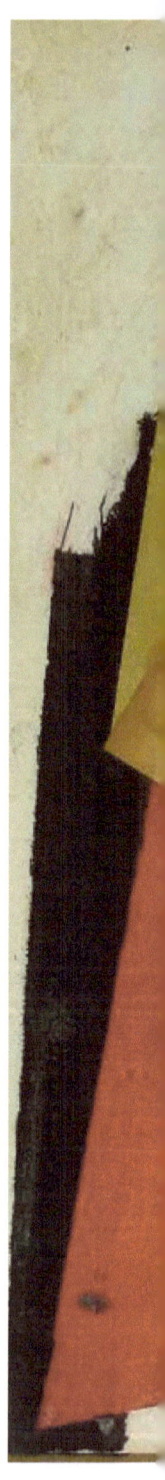

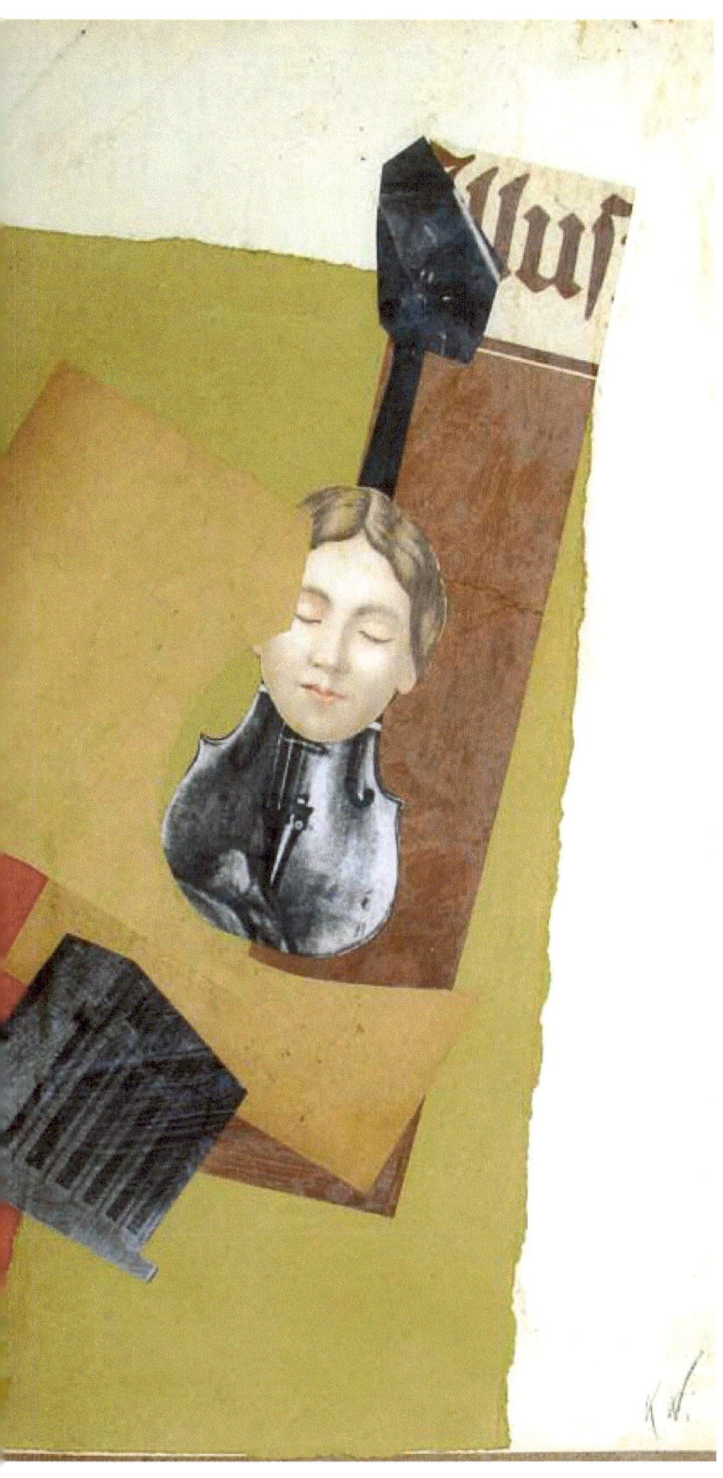

"You have now reached a stage where teacher and pupil are no longer two persons, but one. You can separate from me any time you wish. Even if broad seas lie between us, I shall always be with you when you practice what you have learned. I need not ask you to keep up your regular practicing, not to discontinue it on any pretext whatsoever, and to let no day go by without your performing the ceremony, even without bow and arrow, or at least without having breathed properly. I need not ask you because I know that you can never give up this spiritual archery. Do not ever write to me about it, but send me photographs from time to time so that I can see how you draw the bow. Then I shall know everything I need to know."

Eugen Herrigel

IARFHOCAL ★ AFTERWORD

The images in this book are disturbing, collages from tumultuous times in a Europe ravaged by war and genocide. We can never say for sure that the evil of Nazism and Stalinism has been exorcised, never to return again. Can we?

Karl Waldmann's collages—I have no comment to make on their provenance—hit me like a bolt out of the blue. I had been writing ekphrastic haiku in Irish and English, spontaneous responses to works of art; the artwork, mainly of Impressionists, and the haiku seemed to be suffused with light and goodness—and then I came across these collages almost accidentally. I had to respond. There was something to exorcise, if not in my being, personally, then most certainly in the collective being. The 21st century, Europe once again was crawling with displaced people—men, women and children.

Nothing is accidental. As soon as I saw them, I knew I would respond with a hundred or so haiku, not knowing what might be dredged up. Emaciated inmates in a concentration camp, in strong contrast to the well-nourished men and women of the master-race, these and other images contrasted starkly with what I had been only days before imbibing, Impressionists, Realists and Romantics with their haystacks, sunflowers, moonlit lakes and so on. But haiku at its best is a non-dualistic art and flourishes not on Fancy but on what is Real. In haiku, all is gist to the mill.

I hadn't lived through the Nazi or Stalinist era but my father had served in the Wehrmacht. At a very early age, schooled by nuns, I had discovered a prayer by St Teresa of Avila, 'Let nothing disturb thee'. Later I discovered the wisdom of the East and looked forward to the next edition of the *East-West Journal*. The German philosopher Eugen Herrigel appeared to me to be one of those Westerners capable of straddling East and West, as Alan Watts did. It came as a bit of a shock to discover their feet of clay, Watt's alcoholism, Herrigel's Nazism. A rabid Nazi he was not, but certainly a Mittläufer or fellow-traveller.

I have peppered this book of haiku and senryu with quotes from Herrigel whose *Zen in the Art of Archery* hit the mark for me and, no doubt, for thousands of others. How can I reconcile his spiritual insights with his Nazism? I can't. That would be the easy answer. Do you want the difficult answer? The difficult answer is that I can. In a strange way, everything must be reconcilable or we are at constant war with ourselves and with others.

Throughout this book of haiku and senryu, you will hear the repeated trope, 'Kind sir', as though a hungry orphan in a Dickensian novel were looking for some act of kindness, hoping for a random act of grace. That voice is the child's voice in the author, the child-man grappling with evil that seems almost beyond understanding. There are exploitative images of women among these collages and I found myself looking for images of my own mother among them to counteract that effect, somehow, and to see goodness and truth glowing behind the twisted, denatured world portrayed.

I hadn't thought of Herrigel—and the paradox he represents—for over forty years. Many paradoxes surround him. It took him a whole year to learn

how to breathe as a Master Archer must breathe
—and he eventually dies of lung cancer. That
sounded paradoxical to me. Or ironical? There were
seeming paradoxes all the time in conversations
with his Master:

How can the shot be loosed if 'I' do not do it?
'It' shoots, he replied.
And who or what is this 'it'?

These questions and answers about archery strike
as well at the heart of haiku! Three years after
this conversation, Herrigel found the answer when
the arrow released itself!

Gabriel Rosenstock

other haiku collections from The Onslaught Press:

behind the yew hedge (2015)
Gabriel Rosenstock & Mathew Staunton

Antlered Stag of Dawn (2015)
Gabriel Rosenstock, John McDonald, & Mariko Sumikura

Tea wi the Abbot (2016)
John McDonald & Gabriel Rosenstock

and from our friends at Evertype:

The Naked Octopus (2013)
Gabriel Rosenstock & Mariko Sumikura

*Fluttering their way into my head:
an exploration of Haiku for young people* (2014)
Gabriel Rosenstock

.